'If I were rain, I would go where water cannot be found.'

Rani, 12 years

Third edition
Title Sponsors
Avantha Group
Oracle India Pvt. Ltd.
Photolink Creative Group
The Sona Group

Associate Sponsors
Kavita and Arjun Singh
Ireo Management Private Ltd.
P.S.Bedi Group

Previous editions
Title Sponsors
AIS Glass
Ballarpur Industries Ltd.
Punj Llyod Ltd.
The Nand and Jeet Khemka Foundation

Associate Sponsors
Benu and Ramji Bharany, Divya Kashyap;
IDP Education Australia, Interglobe;
Jane Blaffer Owen, Mona Schwartz;
Niraja Nanjudan, P.S.Bedi Group;
Rotary Club of Delhi Southend;
Sandeep Mani, Sona Koyo Steering Systems Ltd;
Tanya and Arvind Dubash;
Zuber Aria

Special Support
First City Magazine
Thomson Press

Our deep gratitude to the Khemka family for their enduring support.

If I were rain

CELEBRATING THE SPIRIT OF INDIA'S DISADVANTAGED URBAN CHILD

a youthreach initiative

Edited by Nanni Singh

Photography edited by Prabuddha Dasgupta

Editor	Nanni Singh
Photo Editor	Prabuddha Dasgupta
Book Design	Anjila Puri
Associate Editors	Charlotte Dugdale; Teena Ray
Fundraising	Sophia Cunningham
Special Advisors	Devika Singh; Jaya Srivastava
Editorial Consultants	Amar Behl; Prabhat Kumar Jha
Art Facilitators	Manjari Sharma; Sheyna Baig; Veena
Editorial Partner	Ankur Society for Alternatives in Education, New Delhi
Research and Translation	Ankita Anand; Anushree Somany; Asha Narayan; Gauri; Kavita Charanji; Lara Shankar; Mahuya Banerjee; Niti Sabharwal; Niraja Nanjudan; Ritu Singh; Sharat Bhagat; Shalini Sharma Rattan
Participating Organisations	Ankur Society for Alternatives in Education; Butterflies; Deepalaya; Hope Project; Karm Marg; Nanhi Kali; Navjyoti Delhi Police Foundation; Project WHY; Salaam Baalak Trust; Very Special Arts
Photography	Achinto; Amit Khullar; Anita Khemka; Arun Ganguly; Azad A Bhutia; Charudutt Chitrak; David de Souza; Dayanita Singh; Fawzan Hussain; Gurinder Osan; Jason Taylor; Manish Swarup; Manoj Jain; Neeraj Paul; Nitin Upadhyay; Pablo Bartholomew; Photo Ink; Sanjay Acharya; Sanjoy Chatterjee; Santosh Verma; Swapan Parekh; Tarun Chhabra
Cover Photograph	Manoj Jain

Text Copyright © Youthreach
Photography Copyright © Individual photographers as listed on page 303

Published 2003 by Youthreach
Second edition 2005
Third edition 2008
11, Community Centre Saket New Delhi 110017 India
Phones 91 11 26533530/26533525/ 41649067 Fax 91 11 26533520
yrd@youthreachindia.org www.youthreachindia.org

Printed by Thomson Press, New Delhi, India
ISBN 81-7525-444-0

contents

About three years ago, three charming, young women came to see me in my home in New Delhi. They represented an organisation called Youthreach, and wanted to do a project on urban street children. The idea was to give these children a platform to be seen and heard, something that they had never had. What they were asking me was this: would I take on the colossal task of photographing the entire content of the book, spend about a year in doing so, put my significantly more lucrative commercial work on hold and of course get paid a pittance for the effort.

The idea terrified me.

Firstly, I was not that kind of photographer. I have always been shy of entering universes that I have no understanding or experience of, and fire away like a trigger-happy tourist. Secondly, I was sure that there had to be a treasure-house of already existing images, shot by photographers across the country, who had a far greater understanding of the subject than I. It would be a shame to ignore that body of work and start afresh. Lastly, I also knew that this project would be all consuming, and to do it justice I would have to put the rest of my life on hold, something that I was not prepared to commit to at that point of time. Especially without adequate financial compensation.

So I chose the easy way. I agreed to help collate the material, edit it, shape it, and give the project a general visual direction.

Over these last three years, my involvement with the project has been at best, erratic: given to bouts of pessimism, followed by extreme elation; long absences followed by short bursts of furious activity; weeks of slumber suddenly brought to life by a phone call with chest-thumping news; days spent wondering if it was all a waste of time, and if any of it was ever going to see the light of day; and always somewhere deep down the nagging question, why am I doing this, and that too for no money?

So much for the downside. At a more profound, personal level, even with my peripheral involvement, this project was slowly opening up my insides and changing my life forever.

In the first place I was completely taken by the degree of uncompromising commitment brought to the project by the Youthreach team. We all complain about social injustice and the evils of this world, but very few of us get out of our armchairs to do anything about it. We ascribe our apathy to the dearth of time, the pressure to get ahead in a frantic, consumption oriented world, the needs of our immediate families, a growing trend towards an individualistic, insular society, and a burgeoning cynicism towards the possibility of change in a world gone off the rails.

But here was a bunch of young people: sensitive, sophisticated, super-intelligent, passionate, charming and enterprising, who could have chosen to do anything; but instead chose to work for social change.

With good old-fashioned idealism in their heads, fire in their bellies, and most importantly, faith in their hearts. There were many times, for instance, during the making of this book, that I lost heart because no funds seemed to be forthcoming, but their faith was unwavering. "The money will come" I heard Nanni say many times, with a Buddha-like conviction and without a quiver in her voice. And it did. I learnt a lot from them. They helped immensely in restoring my faltering faith in the struggle for change.

Secondly, this project brought me in touch with a goldmine of photographic talent, spread across the length and breadth of the country. Work came in from obscure places, and unheard of names. Committed, socially aware photographers did new work without a fee. Looking at their work I am ashamed that I could have even for a moment considered doing it all myself. These individuals and their talent have humbled, nourished, inspired and energised me, through the making of the book.

And lastly, but most importantly, my connection with the subject of this book, the children themselves, has given me a perspective I never had before. Although my personal interaction with them was some-what limited, I learnt slowly about them and their world through their expressions in interviews, writings, drawings, paintings, poetry and workshops, all of which combined, had the effect of lighting a stick of dynamite under my bottom. In other words I was completely blown away by the spirit of these kids, deprived as they may have been of the material pleasures that we take for granted, but blessed instead with a profundity of thought, feeling and expression that was absolutely mind boggling. These were the same kids that I used to see sleeping on pavements, begging on streets, polishing shoes, carrying bags at railway stations, scrounging in garbage bins; only now I see them differently; I see them as intelligent, intuitive, compassionate, loving, creative, God fearing beings, who just happen to have been born in frugal circumstances.

It has never failed to amaze me that in a society that advocates equal rights for all, there is always an invisible but firm line that separates the 'us' from the 'them'. Only in our case it's not a line but a glass wall. You can see the other reality but you cannot hear it. You encounter it everyday of your life but all you see is a face pressed up against the glass window of your air-conditioned car. You look away hoping the apparition and all it represents, will disappear, which it does the moment the light changes, and along with it goes instantly the whole universe that co-exists with us every living moment.

The following pages will give you a glimpse into that very universe.

Prabuddha Das Gupta

'If I were rain' began its journey more than three years ago, in our office set in the midst of a bustling community centre in New Delhi. As with most other cities in India, ours too has her share of children who live in the fringes of the modern urban wilderness. Mostly termed 'disadvantaged', these children exude easily the quintessential qualities of childhood – warmth, exuberance, a freedom from fear, the purity and wide-eyed wonder at the magic of all that exists. Our work at Youthreach, over the previous years had left us feeling that the way 'disadvantaged' children are understood and indeed 'presented' is at once patronising and unfair. Often as statistics in studies or sponsorship requests, 'disadvantaged' children rarely find the space through which to reveal themselves fully, to speak their minds, tell their stories, reach out to touch…

Any support that has come as a result of creating this inadequate portrayal has been from a standpoint of pity. We felt there was an urgent need to dispel this half story and fill the gaps, to create a window for the light that shines through these children. To ask for support but not from pity – rather from a concern for perfect children in an imperfect world.

'If I were rain' is the result of over three years of intensive work that has taken us through the tricky terrain of very complex issues that a project of this nature entails. The vision at least was clear – the children must speak for themselves. We as adults must only play the peripheral role of facilitating their voices in a way that pulls the whole picture together. What really are the critical issues that affect children? What do the children themselves feel? What are their deepest challenges? Their greatest joys?

Here are children that you see all too often. If you live in a city in this part of the world, as you drive or ride or walk to work, as you walk in and out of entertainment spaces, your local market, anywhere and everywhere…If you live elsewhere, then you might meet these children through the images on television screens, statistics in reports, sponsorship requests…These are the children you will meet here. Only a little differently, a little closer than you might have expected, a lot deeper than you might have had a chance to, ever before.

The children you meet in these pages are a very small fraction of all those who lead disempowered lives all over India. Unique as every child is, the children of 'If I were rain' are representative of the ten million who live on India's streets and a whole lot more who live in the slums of our urban centres. Their stories are shared, and often untold. Their lives are highly visible yet often unseen.

'If I were rain' hopes to create a bridge between worlds, between the deep divides of economic categories, between the 'believed' and the 'real' workings of lives different than ours. It is an attempt to examine closely the hardship and the joys, the integrity and the exploitation, the strength and vulnerability, the order and the chaos, the frailty and tenaciousness, that is intrinsic in the lives of Indian children who have a highly marginalised existence.

Our endeavour is to tell it like it is, by no means to trivialise the underlying extreme adversity that forms the constant and gruelling background in which these children grow, learn and create. On the contrary, to explore the wealth of intelligence, creativity and joy that exist, despite the adversity. To acknowledge the strength that emerges in the face of homelessness, exploitation, police brutality, demolitions of homes, physical labour and the complete denial of even the most basic rights. To raise the curtain on the totality of that experience, so that the child can be seen whole, not fragmented and cast aside as a mere object to either be ignored or pitied.

In my mind, the single most important reason to have put this book together has been to attempt to restore the dignity that each of these children so richly deserve – not for who they may become in the future, but for who they are now, as they are now. I've never quite been comfortable with that familiar saying of how we must invest in our children because they are our future. I think, on the contrary, that we must invest in them because they are our Now. It is through their 'childness' that we are brought the gifts of wonder and magic, of play and creativity, of nurturing and fearlessness. Of intuitive justice and purity. Of intelligence and courage. Of love.

Children who live in extreme hardship reflect the deepest form of these qualities because the circumstances of their lives carve the spirit through much suffering. Particularly children who run away from home because of abuse or poverty. Even if they live with their families, discrimination is a daily experience for children who live in poverty. If we value childhood at all, we must recognise the traps that lie in the way of all children. To reach out and support, not with the view that these children require the fruitless material excesses that are the backbone of urban existence but to ensure that they have access to basic necessities that will keep them well, to experiences that will nurture a deep sense of self-worth, dignity, the passion to dream, to create, to be whole. Any talk of future is unnecessary if we can acknowledge that childhood is reason enough to extend ourselves. For their sakes and indeed our own.

The book is broadly structured around the framework of the Convention of the Rights of the Child that was adopted by the General Assembly of the United Nations in 1989. The government of India acceded to this convention in December 1992, which means that we as a country are committed to the provision of these rights to all Indian children. It also means that we are accountable to the world community to ensure that these rights are upheld and fulfilled for all children. 'If I were rain' explores four primary rights that are the most critical – Survival, Development, Protection and Participation. To help clarify the context of social 'reality', there is an editorial perspective based on extensive research that forms the backdrop of the children's experiences, their views, and their dreams. Most of the content was gathered through many months of workshops of art and expression.

The process of enquiry was a more intense and in-depth one for the eight children whose stories are presented in detail. Six photographers were commissioned the work of spending a great deal of time with these children in order to capture visually the essence of their lives. All the remaining testimonies, voices and photographs have been gathered from all over the country and put together in a way that most effectively illustrates their message. The book is bi-lingual for obvious reasons – Indian children who have not had access to private education speak primarily in Hindi. It is pertinent to present their voices as authentically as we can, and so I urge you to read through the Hindi as well, even if English is the language you are most comfortable with. Translations have been a massive challenge and I can only hope we've done the transition justice. To actually structure the book, page after page, through a sea of visual and testimonial content, has been perhaps the hardest task and an unrelenting challenge to the mind and heart. My deepest gratitude to Teena and Charlotte, for three years of hard work and infinite patience with the relentless pursuit of deeper dimensions. Sophia for taking on the challenge to fund raise. The Youthreach team, for pitching in, weeding out. Uday, for his quiet constant support. Anjila, for breathing it to life. Prabuddha, for giving it the gift of soul. Bharat, for believing, believing, believing.

To conclude, I would like to address the one question that I have answered many hundreds of times through these years – to sponsors, partners and everyone else whom we consulted for feedback and strength – where will this lead us? Two essays at the end of this book will answer that question very specifically, but for myself, I can only venture to hope that this book sparks the imagination with its light. I hope it enables empathy with the laughter and the suffering contained in its pages. I hope it makes visible to all those who encounter it, the many roads that we can choose to walk when the reading is done, the chapters absorbed. To take that one step towards nurturing the lives of India's millions of children and through that, heal perhaps our own sense of fragmentation and inability to address the deep divide.

'If I were rain' does not seek to change the lives of these children dramatically, only create space that establishes a connection – between our lives and theirs; A space that makes them visible and heard. Where will this lead us?
Perhaps to a bridge between worlds…worlds that exist side by side, yet divided.
An invitation to walk across it for a communion with children we have not known.
And with ourselves, a few shades deeper.

Nanni Singh
Executive Director, Youthreach

INDIA IS HOME TO 400 MILLION CHILDREN, THE LARGEST NUMBER IN ANY COUNTRY IN THE WORLD.

Deepa, 15 years.

'Love is not an object with an ISI stamp that we buy
thinking it will be strong and long-lasting…
Love is a fragrant breeze that touches and passes by,
its fragrance unrecognised.
And sometimes, having felt it,
we still choose to remain strangers…'

'प्यार कोई ऐसी चीज़ नहीं है
कि जिस पर आई॰ एस॰ आई॰ का मार्क लगा है,
जो हमने टिकाऊ और मजबूत समझ कर खरीद लिया।
प्यार तो एक ऐसे खुशबूदार झोंके की तरह होता है
जो कब हमारे पास से होकर गुज़र जाता है
और हम उस प्यार की खुशबू को समझ नहीं पाते।
और कभी–कभी हम उस प्यार की खुशबू को
समझते हुए भी अनजान बने रहते हैं।'

Yashoda, 18 years.

40% OF OUR CHILDREN LIVE IN POVERTY AND EXTREME HARDSHIP.

According to the Government of India, a person living below the poverty line earns less than Rs. 10 per day, or Rs. 296 per month.
The Government calculates that Rs. 10 will buy food equivalent to 2200 calories, which is medically enough to prevent death.

OVER 10 MILLION INDIAN CHILDREN

LIVE, WORK, PLAY, SLEEP, DREAM

ON THE STREETS AND SIDEWALKS

OF OUR CITIES.

'Living on the streets, working everyday.
We have no home, no bed to sleep in.
All that we have is the earth and the sky...'

Chanda, 14 years.

'Life is a riddle
that no one has understood,
because no one knows
what tomorrow holds...
How will it be today?
We are alive this moment,
yet we know not for how long...
There is much happiness
in one moment,
while just the next,
carries so much grief.
And so, life remains
an unsolved riddle.'

Ranjeet, 15 years.

I

SURVIVAL

'If I were rain,
I would go to those who have no water.
I would say to them 'I am coming.'
Everyone on earth would come out
and I would pour water into their
utensils and fill them…'

'अगर मैं बारिश होती,
तो जिनको पानी की ज़रूरत है और नहीं मिलता,
मैं उनसे कहती, 'मैं आ रही हूँ'।
धरती पर, सब बाहर आ जाते तो,
मैं बारिश बरसाती, उनके बरतन भर देती।'

Sumitra, 12 years.

Sumitra, 12 years.

Multitudes of children live in slum clusters in and around India's cities. Forced from their rural homes by scarcity of money and resources, families come to cities in search of livelihood. Here they set up homes wherever they can, with basic available materials.

THE RIGHT TO SURVIVAL

Every child has the right to life

and to the needs that are most basic to existence.

For children to survive they have the right to

shelter and spaces of refuge, food and nutrition,

water and sanitation,

health and medical services,

roads and infrastructure for access to facilities.

Above all, to survive,

children must have the love, protection and commitment of adults.

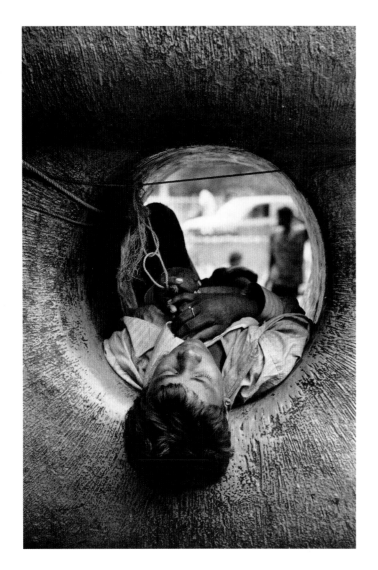

The challenges of survival in India's cities are manifold.

Mothers lack facilities for giving birth safely and are often compelled to return to work within three weeks of their children being born. One in two children are malnourished, increasing their susceptibility to disease and disability.

Treatment for sickness is not easily accessible – lack of investment in medical infrastructure and a huge increase in the cost of drugs has put proper healthcare far beyond the reach of most of these children.

Children living on the street are particularly vulnerable.

'My father pulls a cycle rickshaw.
He spends all his money on alcohol,
meat and *ganja*.

I left home because my father used to
beat me at the smallest of mistakes.
If my mother said anything, he would
beat her as well.'

Suresh, 13 years.

EVERY DAY MORE THAN 50 CHILDREN

ESCAPE INTOLERABLE CIRCUMSTANCES AT HOME

TO BEGIN NEW LIVES ON THEIR OWN

ON THE STREETS.

Children who live on the street have the least access to shelter, nourishing food and healthcare. They work for long hours during the day and at night. Underpaid and underfed, they are most exposed to exploitation and prejudice.

Girls living on the street are the most vulnerable. Most disguise themselves as boys and live in gangs with them. Even before reaching adolescence many of them will be forced into the sex trade.

'Perhaps because our clothes are dirty
most people think of us as thieves and
don't allow us to carry their luggage.
We work as *coolies* despite being beaten
by the policemen and older porters.
We try to protect ourselves from them
and work because we have to feed
ourselves.'

'हमारे कपड़े गंदे होते हैं शायद इसी कारण
आम लोग हमें चोर समझते हैं और हमें अपना
सामान नहीं उठाने देते हैं। हम पुलिस और भाड़े
वाले कुली की मार के बावजूद भी कुली का
काम करते हैं। उनसे बच कर हम काम करते हैं
क्योंकि हमें पेट के लिये कमाना होता है।'

Rakesh, 10 years.

Picking rags, polishing shoes, working in food stalls, mechanic shops and marriage celebrations are ways in which these children earn a living in cities.

'We take care of ourselves by working
on the streets, not by stealing or begging.'

Santosh, 13 years.

A CHILD WHO SELLS RAGS AND WASTE IN DELHI EARNS ABOUT RS. 50 A DAY.

Children living on the street would rather work to earn their living than beg. Only one in ten children take to begging as a major occupation.

'About three or four years ago we faced a severe shortage of food at home. We did not have enough to eat, so we had to beg and ask for food. On days that nobody gave us food we would have to go to sleep on a hungry stomach. It made me so unhappy.'

Sumitra, 12 years.

'People would ask, 'who are you,
where have you come from?'
I was unable to tell them anything,
because I was a mystery,
even to myself.'

'लोग मुझसे पूछा करते थे,
'तू कौन है कहाँ से आया?'
मैं उन्हें कुछ भी न बता पाया
क्योंकि मैं खुद के लिये अजूबा था।'

Rajesh, 14 years.

MUNNALAL'S STORY

Munnalal, 14 years.

Munnalal was born and raised in New Delhi. Deeply disturbed by his mother's second marriage and frequent beatings by his father, Munnalal ran away from home. He moved from one place to another all over the country, living on railway platforms and the street. He eventually met a social worker who took him to a children's organisation where Munnalal found refuge and support. Here he began a life that he values, living with other children who share similar backgrounds. He presently studies in Class 8 and is committed to pursuing his interests in art and acting. Whenever Munnalal now comes across children who live on railway platforms, he is reminded of his time on the street and he hopes to somehow help them out of their hardship.

My name is Munnalal. I am 15 years old. My friends sometimes call me by different names like 'devil', but my family fondly calls me 'Munna'.

When I was a child I used to steal.

Once I was caught stealing. Two of my brothers, a few other boys and an older man were involved. My father beat me badly and threw me out of the house. I haven't returned home since then.

I stole because we needed money at home. But with God's grace I managed to stop stealing. I lived in Delhi Church for a year; then for 3 years in Bangla Sahib Gurudwara; 3 years in Gurgaon and then a few months at the railway station.

At the Delhi Church I used to study. In Gurgaon I picked rags with some people. In Uttam Nagar I worked in a bulb factory. Once one of the boys burnt his hands with hot glass. After that I left the job.

I was brought to the centre from the station by a *didi*. Now I live here.

I would like to be a bus driver when I grow up.

Munnalal, 14 years.

I have thought hard and then made this drawing.
God doesn't exist in this world. Only books like the Bible talk of God.

Munnalal, 14 years.

Whenever I close my eyes, I see layers and layers of love flowing by.

People without homes have so much sadness inside them. From the outside they may seem very happy. Since there is nobody to control them they are kings of their own minds. They make the station, gurudwara, church, *Hanuman Mandir* their home, and spend their lives there.

जिनके पास घर नहीं होता वे अन्दर से बहुत दुखी होते हैं। बाहर से वे बहुत खुश लगते हैं क्योंकि उन्हें रोकने वाला कोई नहीं होता है। इस कारण अपने मन के राजा होते है। वे स्टेशन, गुरुद्वारा, चर्च और हनुमान मन्दिर में अपनी ज़िन्दगी बिताते हैं। ◼

SHEKHAR'S STORY

Shekhar, 15 years.

Shekhar was born and raised in a village in Bihar. Due to emotional and physical violence, he ran away from home. Adapting to the rigours of life on city streets, he found employment as an alcohol seller. Following the arrest of his partner, he decided to try living within the more stable confines of a shelter run by a children's organisation. It is here that Shekhar now goes to school and is pursuing his interests in acting, songwriting and poetry. He dreams of producing a music album someday. During the last few years he has gone back to see his family several times, but chooses to continue living at the shelter. Shekhar has promised his father, with whom he shares a special relationship, that sometime in the near future, he will make a good living and support his whole family.

My name is Shekhar. I would like to
be a hotel manager when I am older.

After running away from home I came
straight to the station. There I sold liquor
with an uncle. We would have to bribe
the police. I was under no pressure at all
from anyone. Uncle treated us well.

At home my mother would beat me
because I didn't study, but at the station
there was nobody to say anything to me.
I was totally free. I feel that the way
I have spent my life there was quite
comfortable and I almost got used to it.

I like wearing jeans and t-shirts because I look quite good in them, compared to other clothes.

Amongst older people, my father is my only friend.

He used to work away from home but would visit us often. He lives at his place of work. He became my friend during a fair at Kalyanpur village:

I was about to eat *gulab jamuns* that I had just bought from the sweet shop when Papa stopped me and said, 'Shekhar you are very stupid.' I asked why… my father said, 'Look, there are flies everywhere. You should know this – flies sit on dirty things and then land on the *gulab jamuns*. Their germs are transferred onto the sweets and you are trying to eat the same *gulab jamuns*! You will fall ill!' Then I told my father, 'Papa, instead of scolding me you explained it to me as if you were my friend.' And my father said, 'I am your true friend. Didn't you know that?' I said no. My father offered me his hand and said, 'Well, my name is Mohan Saimi, I am an engineer and I would like to make friends with you.'

I shook his hand and we became friends.

I used to laugh and share jokes with my father. Now I live at the centre away from him.

Here I laugh and play and sing with my friends in the same way. I love my father the most because he is the one person who understands my problems and has never made me feel like, 'I am your father and you have to do whatever I say.' Instead, he explains everything to me in a loving way. He would say, 'I am your friend. Tell me your problem.'

Maybe that is why I love my father the most.

Shekhar, 15 years.

I believe that nature is God
because the sun, air, water, plants
and trees are our main source of life.
If there were no trees,
where would we find oxygen?
If there was no sun, the whole
world would be in darkness.

And the way they show gods in TV
serials is not true; they are only actors
playing roles. I have heard, as well as
seen on TV, that *Pavandev* is the god
of air and *Suryadev* is the sun god.
The place where gods live is peaceful,
unlike the din in which we humans live.

In our country, violence occurs for all kinds of reasons, in all kinds of places.
Since people support violence, they themselves are responsible for its outcomes -
good or bad. People tend to choose violence in trying to resolve problems.
This is because, since they were born they have seen 95% violence and 5%
ahimsa. Violence is mingled in their blood and they turn to it for the
smallest reasons.

You cannot say violence is right or wrong.
It is an important lesson, and without learning it, we cannot pass the test of life.
Or maybe we don't want to turn away from violence and learn the lesson of *ahimsa*,
because we know all too well that learning the lesson of *ahimsa* will mean putting
up with many things in life.

मैं कहता हूँ कि हिंसा का कोई नाम नहीं है।
हिंसा हमारे जीवन का एक ऐसा पाठ है जिसे पढ़े बिना हम जीवन की परीक्षा में पास नहीं हो
सकते या फिर यूँ कहिए कि हम हिंसा के पाठ को बदलकर अहिंसा का पाठ पढ़ना ही नहीं चाहते।
क्योंकि हमें अच्छी तरह पता है कि अहिंसा का अगर हमने पाठ पढ़ लिया तो सारा जीवन सबको
कुछ न कुछ सहन करना पड़ेगा।

बीते दिन और नए सपने

मेरी वह नादानी थी जब मैंने था अपने
घर को छोड़ा, अपनों से था नाता तोड़ा,
तब मुझे अपनों का न आया था ख्याल,
तब मैं अपने आप में था इतना बेहाल।

पर वक्त ने था मुझको ऐसा मारा,
मैं फिरने लगा था मारा–मारा।
तब उस वक्त मुझे आया
अपने घर वालों का ख्याल।
तब मैं उनकी याद में हो गया था बेहाल।

इस वक्त मैं चाहे उनसे कितनी
भी दूर रहता हूँ पर उनसे
ख़फा तो न रहता हूँ।
अब मेरा एक सपना है
कि मैं कुछ ऐसा काम करूँ,
जो गलती पहले मैंने की थी,
उसको भुला कर
जग में अपना नाम करूँ। ▪

CHILDREN WHO RUN AWAY

FROM THEIR FAMILIES OFTEN MAKE THEIR HOMES

IN RAILWAY STATIONS,

SETTLING DOWN WHERE THEY FIRST ARRIVE.

'I arrived here at the station and stayed. I found some friends and food to eat. We work now and then and take a bath once in a while. We spend the money that we earn within the day. This is our home.'

Jwalamukhi, 12 years.

Homeless children brave heat waves, monsoon rains and harsh winters on their own without protection. Heatstroke, fever, coughs and colds are an inevitable part of their lives. Even if they owned umbrellas, raincoats and quilts they would have no place to keep them.

Children living with their families in slum communities are better protected and cared for. But conditions can be bleak. Slums are mostly illegal, with very little infrastructure or facilities. Families lead disempowered lives – often in makeshift homes, without adequate water and sanitation and with limited access to education and medical facilities.

BULLET'S STORY

Bullet, 12 years.

One of eight children, Bullet lives with his family in a single-room house in a large slum community. His family moved to the city from a village in West Bengal, in search of better livelihood. Bullet began his life in the city by picking rags for extra income for the family before he was approached by a children's organisation. He was offered the chance to go to a non-formal school with flexible timings that allowed him to work and learn. His teacher proudly calls him one of his brightest students. Today, Bullet helps his family by working at his father's provisions store and hopes someday to have a store of his own. He dreams of building a home on top of the provisions store for his family.

My name is Bullet. I like my name a lot.

As a child I used to run as fast as a
Bullet motorcycle. I love running.

I go to school. I study in Class 5C.
I also prepare *murrie*. I have to go to
Lal Qila to fetch kerosene for making
the *murrie*.

On holidays, we carry bags of rice up to the terrace to dry in the sun. We sprinkle salt over the rice – without it the *murrie* would taste bland. In the evening we put the rice back into the bags and carry it down.

We all work together to prepare the *murrie* – Ma adds wood to the fire and my brother prepares it. I fill the packets with it. My father weighs them on the weighing scales and then my sister seals them. *Baba* sells the *murrie* at Ganesh Nagar.

In the winter I really enjoy roasting *murrie* over the fire. It keeps us warm and I love it when the whole family sits together around the fire.

In the summer nobody is around; everybody wanders off to sleep under the fan. Our faces perspire and our clothes are soaked in sweat. Our bodies feel salty and burn all over. And my head feels like it is going to explode like a bomb.

There are fights in the family if we fall short of *murrie*. Sometimes when that happens, I don't even eat my food.

We also have a *paan* shop. My brother Shamshudddin sits at the shop. Sometimes I sit at the shop too. My younger brother and sister play around with the other children. Different kinds of people come to the shop and buy various things like coconut oil, tea leaves, *paan*, Parle-G biscuits, tobacco, Shikhar *gutka*.

84

I like running and exercising.

I like to wear my school uniform
and my *Id* clothes.

I like to study.

I like looking after my pigeons
and going to my village.

I want to become a soldier
when I grow up.

At home I love my parents the most.
Then come my younger sister and
brother.

I love the pigeons even more.

Bullet, 12 years.

If a stranger comes to my house then
I feel shy talking to him because I have
never met him before.

If a friend comes over while I am eating
at home, I feel embarrassed because
I have not eaten in front of him before.

At home I really enjoy it when the whole family is together, when we all sit and watch TV. It is nice when everyone has taken a bath and we sit together on the terrace.

If I fall in love with a girl, I will meet
her for two or three days to begin with.
Then I will ask her to marry me.
If she agrees to marry me, I will send
Ma to speak to her father. After that
I will marry her and start a new life
with her.

जब मुझे किसी लड़की से प्यार हो जाएगा तो
सबसे पहले मैं उस लड़की से दो तीन दिन
मिलूँगा। उसके बाद मैं उससे शादी की बात
करूगाँ। जब वह लड़की मुझसे शादी करने को
राज़ी हो जाएगी तो मैं उस लड़की के पिता से
शादी की बात करने के लिए माँ को भेजूँगा।
उसके बाद मैं उससे शादी करूँगा और फिर मैं
अपनी एक नई ज़िन्दगी बसाउँगा।

When I get angry and try to leave the house, my father catches me and beats me badly. When he hits me like that, I feel unhappy and want to run away from home. But the thought of getting beaten again stops me from running away.

Bullet, 12 years

If we go to some place
and someone catches hold of us and beats us,
Allah comes to save us in the form of a tiger.
So we think of the tiger as God. ■

Children in slum clusters and *bastis* live without a sense of security and stability. As their homes are mostly illegal they may face demolition by municipal authorities at any time. Families are then rehabilitated in remote places, severing them from the social, economic and educational lifelines, so essential for their well-being.

'In July 2000, government officials came to survey our area. They gave us no details but we soon realised that we would not have homes to live in, in a few months time, maybe even a few days. No one was given a notice.

We were very afraid. It was a question of our lives, our security and our education. We spent all our nights sleepless and our days discussing the time when 'they' would come and uproot our homes.

What would happen to people's work and livelihood? We had built our homes after years of hard work. Would we ever get over the pain of seeing them being broken to dust?

We were asked to leave our homes the day before *Diwali*. Three people from the Municipal Corporation arrived and declared, 'Empty the *basti* or else we will bulldoze it.' We were so afraid of the bulldozers, we started pulling down our own homes. There was no other way to save our belongings.

I felt like breaking the head of the bulldozer man, but then I thought he is human too.'

Sunita, 12 years.

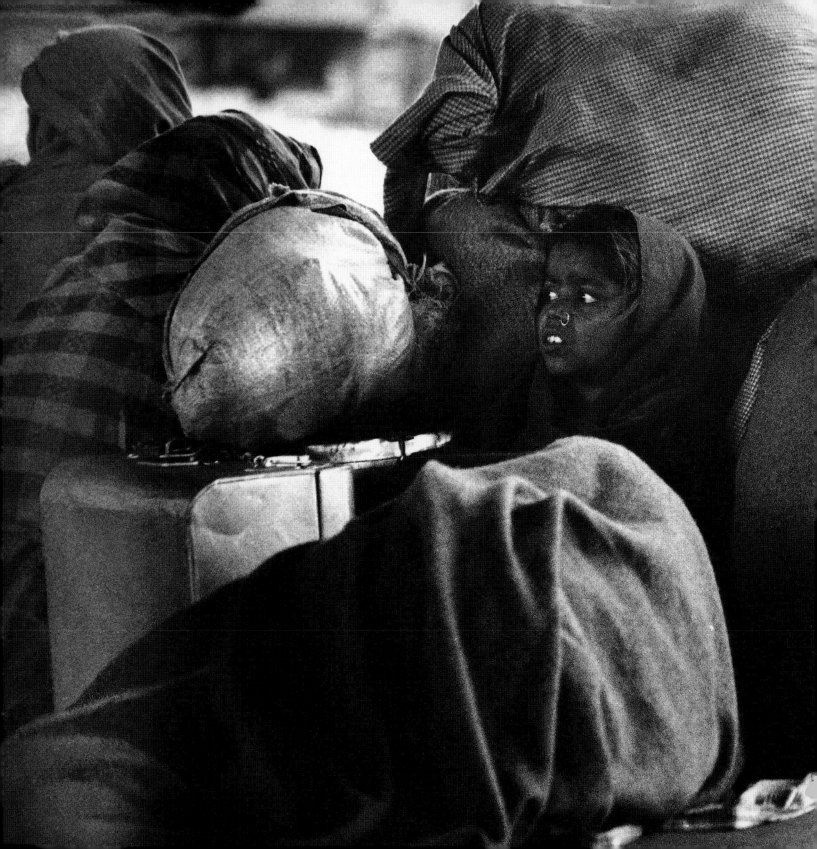

'Please stop! Don't crush our homes.'

'रुक जाओ, हमारे घर मत रौंदों।'

Dilshad, 11 years.

Zubaid, 12 years.

'This world belongs to all of us.
Why do you ask whose land it is?
Come, let us get together
to fight for our rights.
We don't fight for power
for false fame or glory.
We fight together
for our homes and families,
for our jobs and facilities,
for the education and health
of our children,
for our respect and dignity.'

Jayanti, 14 years.

'If I were rain,
I would pour down on the shrubs and plants
that have dried. Birds would sing, flowers bloom,
plants and trees grow fresh with new leaves
and bear fruit.'

'अगर मैं बारिश होती,
तो मैं सूखे पेड़ पौधों पर गिरती
और पक्षी चहचहाते।
फूल खिलते और पेड़–पौधे घास,
फूल पत्तियाँ खिल उठतीं।'

Meenu, 12 years.

Meenu, 12 years.

II

DEVELOPMENT

Every child has the right

to explore and express her deepest potential.

For children to manifest this potential,

they have the right to informative, academic and creative learning,

play and leisure,

and exposure to culture and diversity.

All children have the right

to relationships and experiences

that enrich their lives,

that provide nourishment for their spirit

and sense of self.

'As we grow aware of relationships,
we begin to sway in their love.'

'रिश्तों की पहचान होते ही हम उनके
प्यार के झूले में झूलने लगते हैं।'

Shahana, 17 years.

'No, love can never be weighed or measured.
Love is like a well of cool water that quenches
everyone's thirst but never dries up.'

'नहीं, प्यार को तोला नहीं जा सकता क्योंकि
प्यार तो एक ठंडे कुएँ की तरह है जो सबकी प्यास
बुझा देता है लेकिन खाली नहीं होता।'

Yashoda, 18 years.

'Money is a thing that comes and goes.
But true friends are not sold in the
market. They are gifts from God,
granted to us because of who we are,
or our good fortune.'

'पैसा तो आने–जाने वाली चीज़ है,
लेकिन सच्चे साथी बाज़ारों मे नहीं बिकते।
ये तो भगवान् की एक ऐसी देन है जो हमारे
स्वभाव या खुशकिस्मती की वजह से हमें
मिल ही जाते हैं।'

Yashoda, 18 years.

'Friendship is very important in one's life. There is no life without a friend.'

Tabassum, 13 years.

'Within this huge world man creates a small world of his own that he calls family.'

'इंसान इस दुनिया में अपनी एक छोटी सी दुनिया बनाकर रहता है जिसे वह परिवार का नाम देता है।'

Neelofar, 15 years.

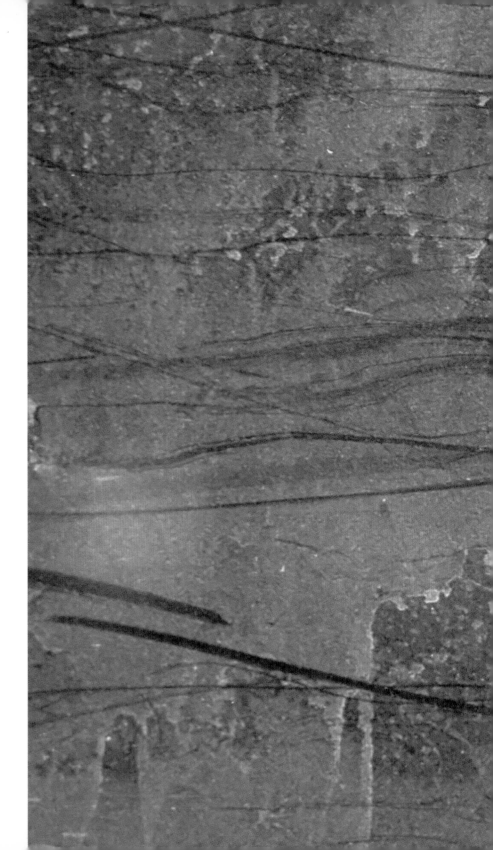

'In our daily lives we share all
our joys and sorrows with others.
We live and die with them.

And there are times
we need our solitude and silence.
But when our solitude becomes
too much, we tire of it
and seek change.

That is when we realise
we can live without solitude,
but we cannot live
without everybody else.'

Yashoda, 18 years.

'When I was young I loved watching kites soar in the sky. I used to think that I could also fly by holding on to the kite's string. That's all I could think of.

One day while playing by the road, I caught sight of a kite flying. The kite had broken off and its string was floating in the air. It was as if lightning struck me and at that moment I wanted nothing but to fly like the kite. My mind was on fire. I rushed blindly towards the string, not realising it was in the middle of the road. As I reached for the string, a three-wheeler rammed so hard into me that I didn't know where I was.

As I rubbed my eyes open, I found my *Dadaji* seated next to me. He asked, 'Why were you playing on the road? What if something had happened to you?' I replied, '*Dadaji*, I was thinking of flying in the sky. How did I know that a three-wheeler would hit me?' When *Dadaji* heard this he took me in his arms and pulled me close, saying, 'You can't fly in the sky by holding on to the string of a kite. You have to sit in a helicopter to fly in the sky.'

That was it. That day my desire to fly by a kite string disappeared, but in its place a burning desire to fly in a helicopter was born.

This wish has remained till today.'

Yashoda, 18 years.

Dhanraj, 15 years.

118

'Our elders are an indispensable part of our lives. They are like a roof over our heads. They take responsibility for our sorrows. They are a refuge.'

Shahana, 17 years.

'It is said that a person who loves
another will find herself standing
first at the threshold of God's home.'

'प्यार कोई इंसान से करता है
तो कहा जाता है कि खुदा के घर
वह सबसे आगे खड़ा होगा।'

Azra, 16 years

YASHODA'S STORY

Yashoda, 18 years.

Yashoda lives with her family, in a *basti* in the heart of a city. Very closely knit with her family, she has faced much hardship at a young age. Married as a child, she lost her six-month old baby to a fatal incident. Having left school at Class 8, Yashoda now lives at home and is intent on rebuilding her life. She has been part of a creative computer programme run by a children's organisation in her locality and is one of a team of young people that produce a community newspaper called *Ibarat*. Besides honing her own skills at the computer centre, Yashoda teaches other children and earns a stipend which adds to her sense of self-sufficiency. She says the computer centre has enriched her life by rekindling her faith in people and providing her with the opportunity to make friends.

I am Yashoda and I am 18 years old.

A lot of people compliment me when I wear new clothes. But I think it's not me, it is the *salwar kameez* that looks good on me. I am of medium height, have a round face with sharp features. I was quite fair but I am growing darker by the day. I have long hair. I am neither fat nor thin.

I have a strange habit. I cannot bear people doing anything wrong and can't stop myself from pointing out their mistakes. I am not saying that I don't have any shortcomings. In fact I believe that it would be hard to find another person with as many faults as me.

But what do I do about my sharp tongue? It doesn't refrain from pointing out others' mistakes. My harsh words hurt the other person like sharp thorns in the eye.

Come, let me introduce you to every member of my family.

This is my *Chachaji*. Now you will wonder why I am going to tell you about my *Chacha*. That is because we call our father *Chachaji*. He works in a bearings factory. After doing backbreaking work from morning till evening he brings home Rs. 50 and that too not every day. He gets it once in two or three days or, when the factory owner is in a generous mood he hands over the money to *Chachaji*. The factory owner is not at all concerned if his workers have enough to eat or not.

Working with such heavy machines, my father has developed a pain in his chest. But at this age what else can he do? He has never learnt any other work. He has spent all his life working on machines.

My mother had wanted him to learn some other work but my father did not show interest in any. If he ever showed any, it was only towards the bearings factory. Now my father wonders why he never learnt anything else. But what is the use of crying over spilt milk?

Now meet my mother. She is 45 years old. My mother is like a raw coconut – hard on the the outside and soft on the inside. My mother was married when she was 15. Since then she has always been working. Earlier, she had the double burden of working outside as well as at home. As we grew up she was relieved of the housework, but she is still not free from the work outside. The day she is relieved of that it will mean the end of our meals.

अगर माँ को बाहर के काम से छुट्टी मिल जाएगी तो हमारे खाने की भी छुट्टी हो जाएगी।

My sister's name is Lakshmi. She is 16 years old. She is very fond of dancing and keeps swaying to songs shown on TV. I feel that she is even better than Michael Jackson. Lakshmi is not as beautiful as her dancing. She left school after Class 9. Everybody advised her to complete her studies but she refused to understand.

Now come, meet the youngest and most adorable, my brother Rahul. He is 14 years old. Being the only son in the family he is a favourite with everyone. He was never interested in studies and so he dropped out of school after Class 5. Ma and *Chachaji* explained to him, '*Beta*, we are uneducated. At least you should study.'

Even as a child Rahul was very restless. He was always busy playing, so Ma and *Chacha* found him a job as a jewellery box maker. On Sundays, his only day off, he always plays cricket at Nehru Hill Park.

His dream is to become a great cricketer. But we tell him, 'Cricketers are well educated and speak English fluently. You can't even speak Hindi properly – you use factory language.' On hearing this he gets irritated and we get into long arguments.

Whenever I am alone at home I feel very sad. I feel as if the walls are closing in on me.

I don't like being at home by myself because I am so used to living with people. Most people say that you come into this world alone and you will leave it alone.

I wonder – how can we be alone when we are surrounded by people? As soon as we are born, our parents introduce us to a web of relationships.

Families share their joys and also their difficulties. Five fingers, when gathered together, make a fist. So, when members of a family live together with love, the strength that comes from it is enough to see them through any challenge. But if there is disharmony, then it is more like being in a *dharamshala* – an experience in which people live together, but as strangers to one another.

जिस तहर पाँच उँगलियाँ मिलकर घूँसे का रूप ले लेतीं हैं, उसी तरह परिवार के लोग भी अगर मिलजुलकर और प्यार से रहें तो दूसरो के लिए चुनौती साबित होते हैं। लेकिन अगर कहीं इसमें फूट की दीमक लग जाए तो यह परिवार नहीं बल्कि धर्मशाला बन जाती है। जिसमें लोग रहते तो हैं मगर एक–दूसरे से अनजान।

I can never forget the darkest day of my life – 16th August.

My son Kunal was admitted in ward No.18 at Irwin Hospital. His condition was very serious.

The doctors told us to arrange for blood. At the time my mother and I were the only ones at the hospital. We called home to inform them about Kunal's condition.

Soon all our relatives arrived at the hospital. My mother told them that the doctors had asked for blood for Kunal. A small bottle of blood would cost Rs. 2000. As soon as they heard the amount they behaved as if they had been born deaf and dumb.

That is when I realised how a crisis situation could turn relatives to strangers. The indifference on their faces made me want to scream out to God, who seemed to have turned a blind eye towards me.

Fortunately, my friend Shahana arrived at that very moment. She heard Kunal needed blood and she ran to arrange for it as if it wasn't my child but hers who needed it. When everyone had left us helpless, Shahana came to our rescue. She even managed to arrange for the blood. But it was too late...

I lost the most priceless treasure of my life. I felt as if there was nothing left to live for. I was deeply hurt and the wound refused to heal. It was Shahana who applied the balm lovingly. Without me realising it, she touched a chord in my heart and became my true friend.

I am afraid of loving again because I feel whoever I love truly, leaves me and goes away. And I don't want to love again and again and keep getting hurt.

What is the use of showing my love when I will not be able to live up to it? We cannot live our lives according to our wishes; our parents have been given the right to decide our fate. They may make our lives or wreck them, but we cannot even make the slightest sound about it.

True friends are those who steal our sorrows, throw them far away, and shower our world with happiness.

Once as a young child I went with my mother to her place of work. She left me outside and went in to clean the rooms. In one of the rooms I spotted a computer on the table. I did not know it was a computer – I thought it was a TV. I pushed the door open and walked in. I found the room cool while outside it was blazing hot. Standing in there I felt as though I was in heaven. I began to enjoy the coolness, never before had I felt so nice and cool in summer. I stepped forward and started pressing the keyboard buttons.

Suddenly someone from behind caught hold of my hand very tightly. I turned and saw a thin, fair lady. She held my hand and dragged me out of the room. With tears in my eyes I stood outside. My mother came out carrying a bucket of dirty water and a broom in her hand. Seeing her I began to cry. She put aside the bucket and broom and asked me why I was crying. I told her through my tears that I had touched the TV and the woman had sent me out of the room. And I wanted a similar TV right away. My mother tried to quieten me down lovingly but I cried so much that I was red in the face.

This incident always reminds me of the huge and never-ending divide between the rich and the poor. If money causes people who are so close to behave badly with each other, then how can we expect strangers to treat us as equals? ■

ONE OUT OF EVERY FOUR CHILDREN IN INDIA DOES NOT GO TO SCHOOL.

'If we didn't have to work we would study. We would like to study too!'

Shariful, 13 years.

Government figures show one hundred percent attendance at the primary school level. Based on enrolment numbers, this figure does not take into account children who drop out. Children drop out of schools for various reasons: seasonal migration, language difficulties, unsuitable schedules, irrelevant curriculum, demotivating teaching and unwarranted punishment. First-time learners are particularly vulnerable because their parents do not recognise the benefits of literacy.

Children who live on the street may be keen to study. But they have limited access to school and often cannot follow the school timings. Since many of them need to work, they find themselves caught between school and earning.

THE GOVERNMENT OF INDIA SPENDS 18% OF ITS NATIONAL BUDGET ON DEFENCE.

IT SPENDS 3.25% OF ITS NATIONAL BUDGET ON EDUCATION.

60.5% of primary schools in India have no chalk.

65% have no blackboards.

35.2% have no mats to sit on.

50% have no playgrounds.

There is 1 pre-school for every 8000 children.

Across the country, schools suffer from inadequate classrooms, lack of teaching aids, poor teacher training,
and a near absence of libraries, laboratories and sports facilities.

Children require vocational training and life skills along with literacy. Vocational skills to help them find employment and earn a livelihood. Life skills to help them cope with emotional and social challenges.

'May no one be compelled to
hold out their hands in need.
May I have money enough
that I never have to refuse
anyone anything.

May I become so extraordinarily
famous that everyone in the
whole world knows who I am,
and never forgets me.'

'वक्त किसी को इतना मज़बूर न करे कि
उसे किसी के सामने हाथ फैलाना पड़े।
मेरे पास इतने पैसे हों कि मैं कभी किसी को
किसी चीज़ के लिये न नहीं कह सकूँ।

मैं इतना प्रसिद्ध व्यक्ति बन जाऊँ
कि मुझे विश्व में सभी जान सकें और
कभी न भूल सकें।'

Pravin, 18 years.

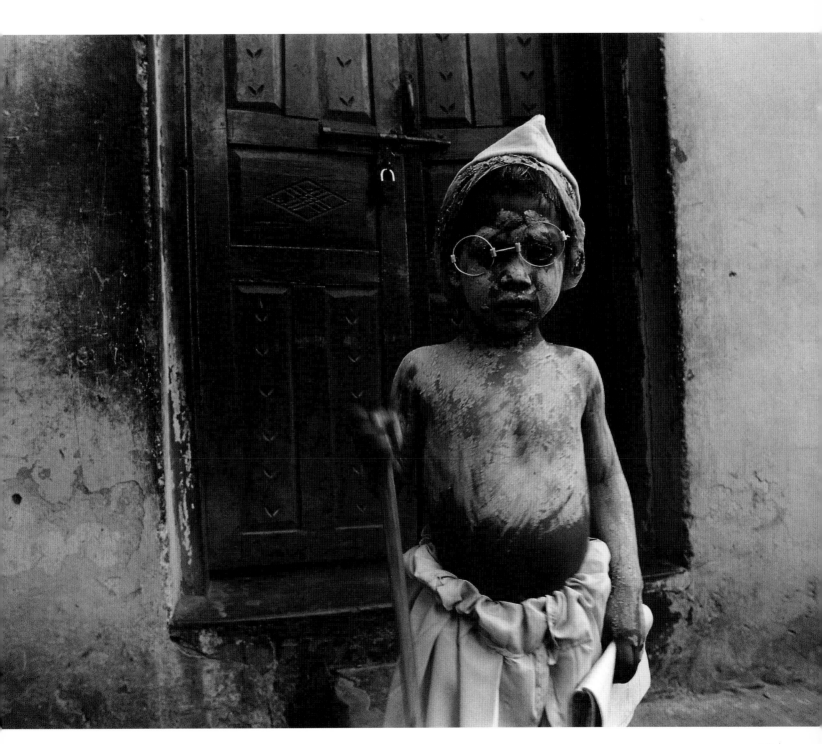

MEENU'S STORY

Meenu, 12 years.

Meenu came with her family from their village in West Bengal, to one of the largest slum dwellings in the city. With her brothers and sisters, Meenu spends most of her day at her grandparents' house while her father drives a cycle rickshaw and her mother picks waste to supplement the family income. The family also makes bangles, necklaces and other trinkets. Meenu studies at a nearby school run by a children's organisation, which she thoroughly enjoys. She looks forward to going to school and learning. She dreams of becoming a teacher when she is older.

My name is Meenu. I like my name.

I quite like the way I look. I have a cut on my eyebrow. My eyes are neither too big nor too small. My hands are small. I am short in height; not tall. My eyebrows are full and heavy. My face is slightly long. One of my teeth is chipped. I like my hair very much. Whenever my mother wants to cut my hair I start crying.

My house is very big. At least 22 people live in my house. There are six rooms with eight windows and seven doors – three rooms on the terrace and three below. The kitchen is separate.
We have two beds and two tables.

There is a small corner in my house where I like to sleep.

There are three taps in my house: one is in the bathroom, the other two are outside. Next to the tap are a few plants – guava, marigold and *mehndi*. The roof is tiled, with bamboos and tin sheets placed underneath. There are two *almirahs*, one in which we keep utensils and the other in which we store food. There are about seven or eight trunks in our house full of clothes and other things.

In my house, light only comes through when we open our doors. In the summer, when there is a power cut, we open all our windows so that air can pass through.

I like festival days very much. That is when all of us go out together.

On other days we just sit at home, get bored and have no fun. During festivals everything seems new. We whitewash and decorate our homes and wear new clothes. On other days, we don't decorate our houses and we wear the same old clothes.

Even holidays are no different – it's the same old *chawal-sabzi*. But on festivals everyone has a lot of money and special food is cooked – *pulav*, *kheer* and *sevaiya*.

त्योहार वाले दिन सबके पास बहुत पैसे होते हैं लेकिन वैसे छुट्टी वाले दिन तो किसी के पास ज़्यादा पैसे नहीं होते हैं।

और छुट्टी वाले दिन वही पुराना चावल—सब्ज़ी बनाते हैं लेकिन त्योहार वाले दिन तो नया—नया खाना बनाते हैं जैसे कि पुलाव, खीर और सेंवई।

My Papa is called Heera Sheikh. He wakes up at six in the morning and goes to ride a rickshaw. When he returns from the market around noon, his face is quite red and he feels tired. He gives Ma Rs.70 for expenses. After Ma has cooked the food he has his lunch and goes off to sleep. Then my *Nana* asks Papa to sit at the shop and so he does. He doesn't really like sitting at the shop. He just sits there for a short while and sells tea. He gets up around three in the afternoon and starts watching matches with his friends. He has two friends, Dilshad and Abdul Khalid. Papa likes films that have a lot of fighting in them.

When customers come to our tea stall, ask for tea on credit and then don't pay up, it makes me angry.

I like going to school the most – more than staying at home. I love studying. But I don't like it when the boys make noise in class. Then I go to the next classroom to study.

When my mother asks me to do some work and I refuse, she picks up whatever is in front of her and hits me with it. When she hits me with a stick, I jump up. It hurts very much.

I feel very happy when I score the highest marks amongst all the students in my class.

When I lived in the village, my friend
Sarjina and I would go to play in the fields.
They were full of cauliflower, cabbage,
spinach, eggplant, peas, tomatoes, gram
leaves and chilli plants. All the plants
were laden with fruit.

We would sometimes pluck and eat the
peas and sit by the bushes. We would
also pluck tomatoes and chillies, cut them
with the ends of *taal* leaves, add salt and
eat. We used to carry salt from home. The
two of us would also pick up grams to eat.
There were even mustard plants in the field.
We would pull them out, wrap them in
towels and thrash them to remove the
mustard seeds.

We also took the goats to graze.
While they grazed, we went and gathered
wood by the river.

I wish I could stay in my village and not
go anywhere else.

I love my village.

At home I like it when it rains but I do not like the muck. I wish it would just rain without creating any mess.

I am standing in a garden.

I love wearing dresses.

I would like to become a teacher when I grow up. ▪

NEARLY TWO-THIRDS OF GIRL CHILDREN IN INDIA CANNOT READ AND WRITE.

'If I were rain,
I would hail on policemen
and hurt them badly,
because they beat children.'

'अगर मैं बारिश होता,
तो बारिश के साथ बर्फ भी छोड़ता
पुलिस के उपर, वह भी मोटा–मोटा,
क्योंकि पुलिसवाले बच्चों को मारते हैं।'

Raju, 12 years.

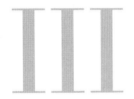

PROTECTION

THE RIGHT TO PROTECTION

Every child has the right to be safeguarded

from any form of neglect, abuse and exploitation.

Children in unusually difficult circumstances

such as refugee children, those involved in armed conflict

and those embroiled in the criminal justice system

have the right to special care.

All children have the right to be protected

from the cruel trap of physical violence, labour and drug abuse.

All children have the right to be protected

from discrimination of any kind.

'Everyone seems to hate us
and perceive us as trouble makers.

Why?
Are we children not part of humanity?
Do we not have two hands, two feet,
two eyes? What evil do they see in us?
We look dirty because of the work
we do, we do not have a home to live
in, a bed to sleep in, we have no one
to take care of us.

Just think.
If we didn't work and earn,
how would we live?
Would we give our lives away?
If any one of us died today,
no one would notice,
no one would ask why.'

Asif, 14 years.

Children who run from difficulties at home have very few safe places to go. There are no safety nets available except for those provided by some children's organisations. The child who reaches the railway station in a big city in India has on an average 20 minutes before encountering some form of abuse or exploitation.

'Wherever and whenever we work,
policemen beat us and make us run around.
People presume we have done something
wrong if they see the police beating us.
Why would they beat us otherwise?

If people would listen to us, they would
understand!'

Sushil, 12 years.

The greatest fear of homeless children across the world is of police brutality.

Children suffer harassment and violence, and are often locked away in jails and remand homes illegally. They are forced to pay much of their hard earned money as bribes to keep themselves out of these 'homes'.

'When I was searching hopelessly
for one square meal a day,
you showed me no sympathy.
When I slept naked, out in the cold,
you kicked and shooed me away.
As I took refuge in your garden in
the rain, you threw dirty water on me.
To wash this dirt off myself,
I took to crime.

Nature left me alone,
uprooted, unsupported.
If you had been there for me,
there would be no need today,
for you to walk in fear
of children who pick pockets.'

Rajesh, 14 years.

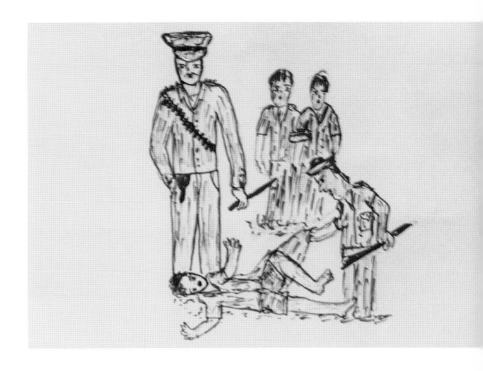

'When children who work honestly for a living are falsely framed by the police, they may go astray. They think if they are beaten without reason, they may as well do something and then get beaten. Children who support themselves honestly shouldn't be harassed by the police. They shouldn't be beaten or scolded, nor accused of being thieves and pickpockets.'

Firdaus, 13 years.

'I have drawn a handicapped man, a policeman and a wealthy man.
He who saves a handicapped man from the clutches of a policeman has God inside him.
I believe God lives in all of us.'

Anuj, 13 years.

'I wonder what the responsibility of the police is?

We are told it is their duty to safeguard the citizens, help them in every social difficulty and stop rising feuds and acts of terror. But until now, I haven't seen the police do any of these things. I have mostly seen them taking bribes.

There is a grocery and tea stall near our house. The owner sells country liquor from his shop, in packets. Each packet costs Rs. 20 – Rs. 25. Someone reported this to the police and a policeman came over. But I wonder what went on between them. Now, the same policeman visits the shop once a week, talks for a while and goes away. The owner pays him a bribe to sell the liquor.

The same policeman once came to our house to have his uniform stitched. My *Ammi*, Papa and the policeman joked and chatted for a while. He asked Papa to stitch a pocket in his trouser. *Ammi* said, 'Is it to keep all the money that you take from the people?' The policeman replied, laughing, 'Yes... It is only with this money that my household runs. Otherwise...' '

Neelofer, 15 years.

'On the New Delhi railway station,
have you seen the children who sift
through waste, do drugs, polish shoes
and who knows what else?
Have you seen all this?

If you have seen them,
have you ever given any thought
to who they are, to their future,
that they are children too,
they have dreams too.
But will those dreams ever come true?
Or is it on the New Delhi railway station
that their dreams will shatter?

Why does this happen to them?
If you have never thought about this,
please think now.
Please save their future
from being destroyed.'

'अगर आपने उनको देखा तो क्या
कभी उनके लिए कुछ सोचा है?
कि वे भी तो बच्चे हैं,
उनके भी कुछ सपने हैं।
पर क्या वे सपने
उनके कभी पूरे हो पाएँगे?
या फिर नई दिल्ली रेलवे स्टेशन
पर ही सपने उनके चूर–चूर हो जाएँगें?
उनके साथ ही क्यों होगा ऐसा?
अगर आपने पहले नहीं सोचा,
तो अब सोच लो
और उनके भविष्य को नष्ट
होने से रोक लो।'

Shekhar, 14 years.

ABDUL'S STORY

Abdul, 14 years

Abdul is a physically challenged child, from Ahmedabad. He ran away several years ago from the growing alcoholism and violence at home. After wandering for a while, he arrived at the railway station in the city where he now lives with a group of children. His parents could never

Abdul is my name.
I am 14 years old.

I live at the station. Here I stay with my friends.
We sleep here, roam around in the coaches,
chat together. I have five or six friends.

Some of them run away, or go to other places,
then I live alone.

Whenever I find some friends...

I come from Ahmedabad.

I went back home once.
My parents asked me, 'Why have you
come home? Why did you run away?'
My father beat me badly.
So I left home.
I ran away again.
I took a train and came to Delhi.
I decided to live here from then on.

I had a friend in Mumbai;
I stayed with him for a few days.
He said, 'We will live in Delhi and
eat well.' So I said okay, let's go to
Delhi. And we came here.
Then he left me.
I stayed at the station and made some
friends. After a few days I liked it.
I decided not to go back home.

If I go home, they will beat me.
I feel afraid.
I will live here at the station...
it is fine.
My friends are here,
I will live with them.

I take solution... I trip on it.
When someone sees a policeman,
everyone runs and they push me aside.

If someone calls me *langra*, I don't answer them.
I don't listen to them at all. They can call me *langra* as many times
as they want. I keep walking further and further away.
Then, as soon as they call me by my name, Abdul, I return.

Older boys say, 'Do you want to see a movie with us... we will give you food and drinks.' Then at night they try to play dirty with us. If we refuse, they threaten us. 'Will you not do it? If you don't, I have older boys in my group. You will not be able to save yourself.'

I like boys who live at the child centre –
they are nice and loving. If people are
nice to me and give me love then I love
them in return. If I had received as much
love at home as I get here... I would not
run away... never run away. At the centre
bhaiyaji tells me that I should stay there
and learn something. I should study.
He says it with a lot of love.
I really like it.

I miss my parents and home when
I see other children with their parents
at the station. I wonder how they all live
together? Wish I too could have stayed
with my parents. Then I would travel
like them. No one would have caught
me. I wouldn't have been beaten either.
Yes, I would've been beaten by my
parents but surely not in the way
the police beat me...

Sometimes I feel like going home
and meeting everyone.

I would go if I had two or three hundred
rupees. But when I have money,
I don't feel like going any more...
Now that I have money, I'll live here.
When there is no money left,
I wish I had not spent it.
I could have sent it home through someone.
Then again, at night I feel had I saved
the money I could have gone home myself.
I would buy clothes for everyone,
have fun and eat well.

But I can't.
I get on a train, go half the way,
and return. I decide not to go home.
I start missing my solution...
Let me have my solution first.
Then I feel like staying where I am.
I go to sleep on the way.

When the train stops, the police come.
They beat and kick me... sometimes they
even lock me up. While they beat me
they say, 'Why are you sleeping here?
Get out of the train.' They chase me
out with their sticks.

If I sleep alone at night I feel lonely.
I cry within. How nice it would have been,
had I stayed at home. I would have
clothes to wear, a bed to sleep in.

I cry... I feel sad. I feel angry with myself.
Had I not left home I would be living
with my parents, playing with my
brothers and sisters.

My friends come. They ask, 'Why are you
crying?' I tell them I am missing home.
They ask, 'Then why did you ever leave?'
I say, I left home... I came here...
but how was I to know that it would be
like this? I feel sad inside.

I think, now that I have left home
I can't go back. If I go home everyone
will ask, 'Why did you run away?
Where were you for so long?'

I feel scared. I feel sad.
Wish I had never left home.
Today, where have I reached...
where do I sleep?

फिर मैं सोचता अब घर छोड़ दिया अब नहीं
जा पाऊँगा। मैं सोचता घर जाऊँगा तो सब
बोलेंगे – 'तू कहाँ भाग गया इतने दिन, कहाँ
रहता था?'

मेरे को डर लगता, उदासी होती।
मन में सोचता – काश! घर नहीं छोड़ा होता।
कितना अच्छा होता। आज मैं ऐसी जगह पर
आ गया – कहाँ सोता हूँ, कहाँ नहीं सोता मैं।

We can't find a place to rest during the day. If we sleep on the platform, the police are on their rounds... they catch us and beat us. They even tear away our blankets. At night, once we are high, we crash anywhere. Where can we sleep in the day?

We keep wandering around... try to catch a minute of sleep while we sit. Or walk with our eyes shut. If the police come we run for our lives because nobody has suffered the kind of beatings we have.

I am very scared of policemen. When a policeman catches me, I start cursing him in my mind, **** why are you catching me? Your children will die. You catch us... but we are like your children. You show off because of your uniform! Without it you are nothing! I keep abusing and cursing him in my mind.

At Dilli Gate, for the smallest mistakes, they take off your t-shirt and beat you. I am scared to go there. I went there once... they stripped me and beat me badly with a belt. Since that day I don't go there. I don't like it.

The police beat... with belts, shoes, hands and fists. Some of them beat with their sticks, some beat with ropes. Some say, 'Tie his hands or he will cry!' Sometimes they gag our mouths. They hit us wherever they like.

They feel, 'How does it matter? These children are good for nothing and should be beaten.' So they start beating us with anything they find.

Vijay has gone to Dilli Gate.
We were sleeping, in the morning…
Vijay was there, Ajay was there,
Allahabadi was there, Mahender too.
All of us were sleeping… First Vijay,
then Ajay, and then Allahabadi were
taken. Mahender got up and said,
'*Bhai*, they have been caught and
taken away!' So I said okay now you
come and sleep here next to me. As he
was sleeping with me, Mahender too
was caught.

And who had them all caught?
Rajender did it for money! He had
all his friends caught. First he took
money from the boys and then he had
them caught. That is why I never
consider him my *bhai*. I had thought
he was a good person.

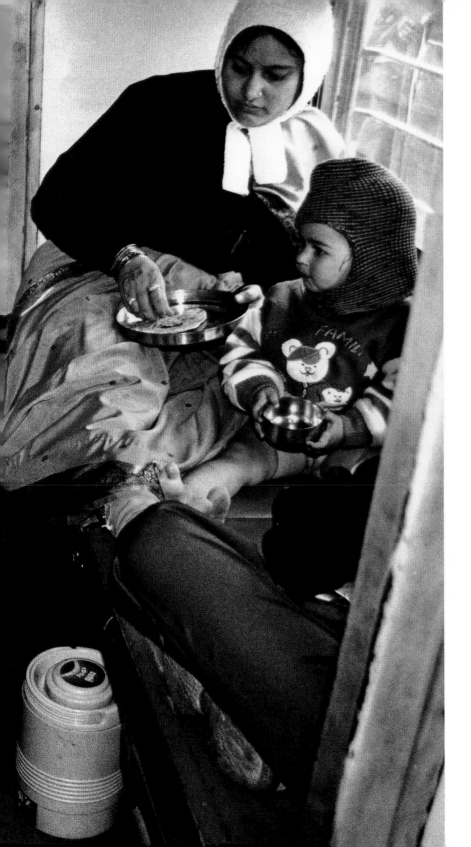

I sleep only after I have had solution. Say twelve or one at night. Then I wake up around six or seven in the morning. I think, I must arrange money for solution now. Then I say, I will do it later when a train arrives. Friends say, 'No, make the money now, before the boys start rummaging through the coaches.' I say, okay, I'll do it now… don't worry. And I make the money early in the morning, for solution. Friends ask me to make some more for tea. I tell them to arrange for tea, I will make money for solution.

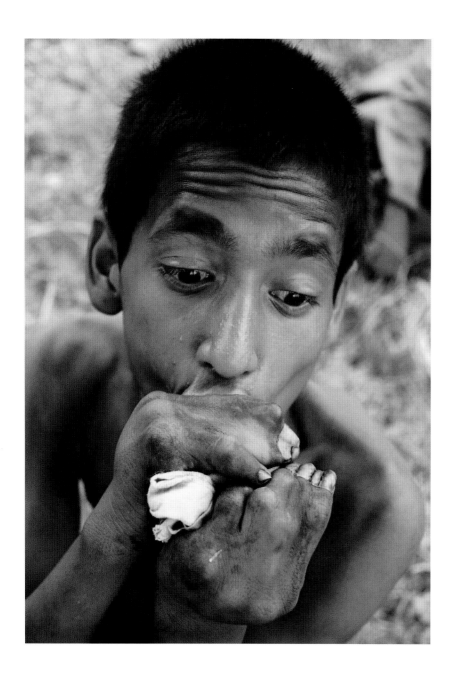

Yes, I trip on solution.
I take about five or six bottles
of solution a day.

I get it from the shop. The shopkeeper
never refuses. He has to earn his money.
Poor guy... the minute I give him the
money, he hands over the bottle
of solution.

You can get two for Rs. 22. If we get
four bottles we can all have it.

We take eight bottles in the day and
eight at night. We just keep inhaling
and inhaling... we never go easy on it.
If I say I've had enough, the others say
'Call for more. We will all have some
more...'

In the morning, even before food, we
take solution. We don't even wash our
mouths. We just sit down and sniff
solution. If anyone's bottle goes missing
he starts cursing the others, '**** why
did you steal my bottle?'

I feel good after taking solution. I enjoy
the high. I don't miss my home anymore.
I just love solution. I don't like doing
any other work... just have more and
more and more solution. I am in love
with the trip.

My best friends?
One is Raju and the other is Bharat.
They are the only two nice boys. They do
a lot for me. Raju always carries me on
his back; he never refuses. But if I make
any mistakes, he curses me. He says he
won't keep me with him. So I say, should
I go away? He says, 'If you leave then
what will I eat?' I say, will you beat me
then? And he says, 'No.'

At the station only one of the boys,
Jwalamukhi, loves me.

He cries if I don't keep him with me.
He lives with me like a brother, loves
me... when I am asleep at night he stays
awake and guards me. He does not let
any one climb up to where I am sleeping.
I like him. Whenever I tell him to get
things for me ... I ask him to get water
and he gets it. Food, and he gets it.
And he gets it fast; he doesn't take time.

Earlier Rajender was also nice. After
he started taking solution regularly he
began to beat everyone. So everyone
is scared of him.

Jwalamukhi has gone...

A friend of mine fell off a train once
when he was going to Mumbai.
He was a good friend. When I was
coming back after three or four days,
he was still there – dried up to his bones.
No one had done anything – dogs were
eating him, flies were all over…
I had to close my eyes.

When I slept at night I dreamt he was
roaming around me. I was scared.
I woke up trembling and remembered
that he was dead. I wondered how his
soul would be feeling?
Where would he be?

I think his soul would have been there…
by the railway track… wandering.
Whenever a train came, his soul would
run away because he would be so scared
of the train.

A person's soul is scared of whatever
has killed him.

At night when I sleep I pray that the
police don't catch me the next morning.
I dream about going back home.
Sometimes I have nightmares of meeting
with an accident on the tracks. I imagine
my body being severed. Once I soiled
my pants because of this nightmare.
I thought there would be blood on the
tracks. But my friends showed me...
there was nothing. They said I had just
had a nightmare.

I don't want to stay at the station...

I always go and watch a movie the day it is released. Even if I have to pay Rs. 150.

I like watching heroes, especially when they fight. My hair doesn't grow like theirs. There was a Sunil Shetty movie I did not like. He wore torn clothes and broken slippers and looked like a madman. So the heroine didn't like him and ran away when he winked at her. In the end he became normal and dressed well.

When I see heroes, I want to be like them, be good and nice... be nicely dressed as well. I like the way they fight and love.

I like this girl, Salma. I want to marry her. Yes I want to marry her when I grow up.

If I marry her I'll make a nice family with her and keep my children well. I will not let them work. If my mother beats my wife, I will stop her... There will be no fights.

I will love my children. If one child hits another, I'll make the other hit him back. That will even out the score and end it. This way I will make sure there is peace at home. If I always love my children, they will not trouble me nor will they fight with other children. And those children will look after my sons when my wife and I are out of town. So if we love them and feed them when they are hungry, they will always want to stay with us.

When I grow old they will feed me. They will take care of me... if anyone fights with me, my sons will stop them.

I don't think about my future.
I hope everything will be all right…
beyond that I don't think.

My friends here at the station love me,
look after me and I look after them too.
If someone beats them, I save them.
I don't let my friends cry.
If anyone cries I comfort him.

Since they love me so much,
why would I leave them? ■

MORE THAN THREE-QUARTERS OF THE CHILDREN LIVING ON THE RAILWAY PLATFORMS USE DRUGS REGULARLY.

'Lately another addiction is catching on – solution. This is a fluid used for correcting writing errors. Children pour it on handkerchiefs and sniff it hard. It is a lethal addiction that causes terrible damage to the lungs. Besides this, many children trip on petrol, diesel and spirit. And some even pop No.10 pills and other sedatives and painkillers. These are easily available from chemists.'

Naveen, 18 years.

'I didn't take any alcohol or drugs earlier in my life. After leaving home, I started picking rags and sleeping on the streets. I would even pick up empty alcohol bottles to sell. I made lots of friends – older, younger and some my own age. Many of them drank alcohol, smoked cigarettes and used tobacco. Others smoked *ganja*. One day a friend persuaded me to try a cigarette saying that nothing would happen. After a few drags I began to feel very dizzy and went to sleep. Soon I started smoking regularly and it quickly became a habit.

In the same way I started drinking alcohol and smoking *charas* and *ganja*.'

Jairam, 15 years.

Drugs offer perhaps the only real escape from the difficult circumstances in which they live. Correction fluid, readily available from stationery shops, is the most common. Children also use alcohol, cannabis and smack.

INDIA IS HOME TO THE LARGEST NUMBER OF WORKING CHILDREN IN THE WORLD.

One in four works hard to eke out a living for themselves or their families in the unorganised sector, in hazardous industries, and as bonded labourers. From *dhabas* and tea stalls to match-making and carpet weaving, children are preferred employees. They are docile, undemanding and can be made to work for long hours with low pay. As many as two million children between five and fifteen years of age work as child prostitutes in India's major cities.

'I took this job for two reasons.
The assurance of a daily meal
and shelter. I work for twelve to
fifteen hours in a day. I earn just
Rs. 100 per month. Usually my
employer does not give me my
full wage as he says he has
deducted some for breakages.

I know I am exploited,
but what can I do?
I cannot read or write and
I haven't learnt any skills.'

Manoj, 15 years.

Rather than helping to alleviate poverty as commonly thought, child labour perpetuates it. Children enter adulthood unprepared, sometimes without even basic literacy and with limited skills. They find themselves trapped with few choices of livelihood and remain working hard for minimal wages for the rest of their lives.

A more positive future for India's working children depends upon putting into place a long-term programme of quality schooling and skills training. We could then prepare to enforce a ban on child labour. It will take all the resources we have at hand – courage, creativity, commitment and funds.

'The call to wipe out child labour all at once doesn't seem feasible to us.

Banning child labour would mean that tens of thousands of families will lose their jobs overnight and become even more helpless.

Instead, the government should first ensure that we are not compelled to work in difficult circumstances.'

Rohit, 15 years.

Mohit, 14 years.

'Twenty million new lives,
Countless builders of the nation,
And yet *Bharat* turns into hell.
Create a new nation
Or keep dying of starvation.'

'दो करोड़ नए जन,
अनगिनत देश निर्माता,
भारत रसातल जाता,
नया राष्ट्र बनाओ,
या भूखे मरते जाओ।'

Dinesh, 16 years.

CHILDREN ARE OFTEN THE LEAST PROTECTED FROM AND WORST AFFECTED BY POLITICAL AND COMMUNAL VIOLENCE.

'The hearts and minds of most people are filled with a hatred that is ready to explode. Like a ticking bomb, this hatred is impossible to diffuse – it is hard enough to even try and touch it. It has become impossible for people from different castes and cultures to live together in peace.'

Neelofer, 15 years.

'The greatest loss is to children.
We are either killed, orphaned
or become homeless and end up
on the pavement.

That is why – no matter how –
governments must put an end
to all wars.'

'सबसे ज़्यादा नुकसान तो हम बच्चों का ही
होता है। हम या तो मारे जाते हैं या अनाथ
हो जाते हैं या बेघर होकर फुटपाथ पर आ
जाते हैं।'

Mehrunissa, 13 years.

'We say God created this world.
Then why do such differences exist?
Some are rich and some poor,
Some are blind, some lame,
Some are beautiful and some ugly.

The way I see it – this is God's violence.'

Shahana, 17 years.

'If you cannot breed love
then do not breed hatred either.
It is strange that most people are
ready to take each others' lives
in the name of God.'

Neelofer, 15 years.

Anil, 13 years.

'There is God but he cannot be seen.
He is in the sky, but he could be closer.
He could be in the sun… he could be in the moon.'

Anil, 13 years.

Naushad, 11 years.

'Allah exists, but he cannot be seen.
He has no legs, no hands, nor a face. Allah is like a black dot.
He can go wherever he feels like, whenever he wants.
No one can ever see Allah. He lives everywhere… mountains, oceans, sky.'

Naushad, 11 years.

'Look around,
people of the world,
these communities are burning.
Enfolded by the smoke of bombs,
little ones are burning.

Voices filled with compassion,
echo on all sides.
Yet they cannot douse the fire.

While little children die,
while little children die.'

Rajesh, 14 years.

RAJESH'S STORY

Rajesh, 14 years

Rajesh has no memories of his parents. He was left entirely alone when his uncle, his sole guardian, was killed. After wandering through the country for a while in search of work and a place to live, a friend told him about a children's organisation that takes care of runaway children. This is where Rajesh now lives and learns. A senior karate black belt, he assists his coach in teaching other children. Besides becoming a karate champion, Rajesh is a particularly gifted artist. His haunting memories find expression through his intense art and poetry.

Rajesh, 14 years.

My name is Rajesh Kumar.
I want to become a karate champion
and make my country proud.
I would also like to become a good artist
and smile like a lotus in full bloom.

233

Rajesh, 14 years.

I have been separated from my parents since I was a baby.
I didn't even know my name.
My uncle gave me a name.
He was a terrorist but I felt really sad when he died.
Since then I have had no one of my own.

There was no love in my life.
Wherever I looked I only saw faces filled with hate.
I used to yearn for love. I never had the love of my parents or relatives.
All I had for a companion was terrorism, a gun in my small hands.

The more I think about my life, I feel like I am in deep sleep...
there is no one to wake me. The fire, the terrorism, the desolate parents,
the innocent children, the burning *bastis*, those screams –
behind every innocent face, hides a devil.

Having seen so much agony, my heart is filled with pain.
I cannot bear to hear other people's sad stories.
Even when I do listen to them, they don't affect me.

हर तरफ़ से चीख़–पुकार सुनते–सुनते दिल में इतना दर्द भर गया कि किसी और की
दर्द भरी कहानी सुनी नहीं जाती। अगर सुनता भी हूँ तो कोई असर नहीं होता।

Fighting and squabbling is something we do everyday.

But I don't want this...

I want peace. I want love. I want unity.

Rajesh, 14 years.

Rajesh, 14 years.

Rajesh, 14 years.

Every time I close my eyes, all I see is my mother's face.

Ma, I miss you so much.
Let me sleep again quietly
and lost in my dreams,
find you there.

Ma, I miss you so much.
My days are spent crying,
my nights, in dreaming.
How do these days
and nights pass?
How is all this time spent?

Where did you go,
so silently, leaving me alone?
Ma, I miss you so much.

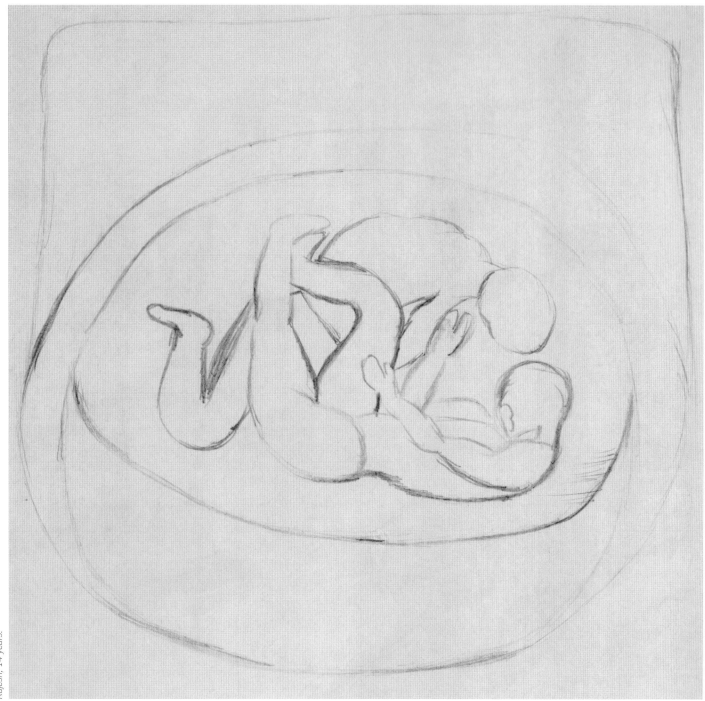

I love my friends because I have never known anything about my parents – where they live, how they live, what they do. Ever since I was a child I have only been amongst friends. All that I know, I have learnt from them. My friends have been with me through good times and bad. I love my friends.

Rajesh, 14 years.

Rajesh, 14 years.

I am afraid of earthquakes. When earthquakes happen, tall buildings seem to fly off,
like bells of wickets, hit by a speeding ball.

Rajesh, 14 years.

My dream is to live in a nice little house with lots of open spaces surrounding it,
where my friends can visit me and we can have fun together.

If I ever fall in love I will consider myself fortunate.
At the crossroads where I find myself today,
I can only dream of love.
This dream is not likely to come true.
It feels like every step is fraught with danger...
I don't know when and where my destiny will lead me,
where it might turn the course of my life.
I know nothing.

अगर मुझे प्यार हो जाएगा तो मैं अपने आप को खुशनसीब समझूँगा
क्योंकि अभी मैं जिस मोड़ पर खड़ा हूँ
वहाँ रहकर मैं सिर्फ प्यार के सपने ही देख सकता हूँ।
यह सपना हकीकत में बदलने वाला नहीं है।
मेरे सब रास्ते ख़तरनाक हैं, पता ही नहीं कि कब किस्मत
मुझे कहाँ ले जाकर छोड़ दे, कहाँ से मेरा रास्ता मोड़ दे,
मुझे कुछ नहीं पता।

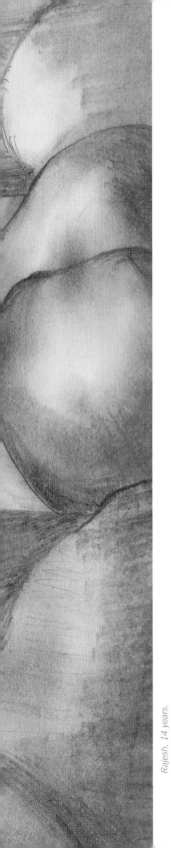

Even today people in our country believe
that God is greater than peace, unity, love and truth...
I say that God exists in these very four words.

We can see him ourselves but we cannot show him to someone else.
We can imagine God in almost anything and find him there.

'Love puts an end to all discrimination.'

'प्यार हर भेदभाव ख़त्म कर देता है।'

Shahana, 17 years.

249

'If I were rain,
all the children would play,
sing and dance with me.'

'अगर मैं बारिश होती,
तो सब बच्चे मेरे साथ खेलते
और नाचते और गाते भी।'

Gulnaaz, 12 years.

Gulnaaz, 12 years.

IV

PARTICIPATION

THE RIGHT TO PARTICIPATION

All children have the right to participate actively

in their communities and nations.

They have the right to express their opinions and be heard

in matters affecting their lives.

It is through this ability to participate, in both the political and personal spheres,

that children will truly find their place in the sun.

It is through participation

that they may reclaim their dignity and freedom from discrimination.

It is through participation

that they may offer their treasures to the world...

'We appeal to everyone in the government as well as society to sincerely plan for our future. Children like us who live and work on the streets, should not be harassed any longer.

We want the next thousand years to help us realise our dreams.
We should not be exploited in any way.
And we should have the opportunity to live a good life free of stress.'

'सरकार एवं समाज सबसे निवेदन है कि हम जैसे सड़क पर काम करने वाले बच्चों के बारे में भी ईमानदारी से कुछ सोचे और करें ताकि हमें अब और सताया न जाये।

हम बच्चे यह चाहते हैं कि आने वाले हज़ार वर्ष हमारे सपनों को रूप देने में सहायक हो। सबसे पहले हम ये चाहेंगें कि सड़क पर रहने वाले किसी भी बच्चे का किसी भी रूप से शोषण न हो और हमें एक तनावमुक्त तथा अच्छा जीवन जीने का अवसर मिल सके।'

Atul, 14 years.

'Nobody listens to these two children.
So they are singing and calling *Shaktiman*.
Shaktiman arrives on hearing their song.'

Raju, 12 years.

In a country like India, children's 'participation' might seem like a luxury. In fact, it is as important a process as meeting children's basic needs of survival, protection and development and should be addressed simultaneously. The more children are heard and engaged with, the more authentic our empathy and ability to contribute meaningfully will be.

'These eyes have a story to tell

They have learned so much,
seen so much joy,
so much grief...

These eyes have known
the heartbeat of love,
a line that divides,
made of blood.

These eyes have contained
the rush of a mother's love,
and rainstorms
pouring hatred.

These eyes have been filled
with oceans of truthfulness,
and the depths
of dark deception.'

Ranjeet, 15 years.

'Look at this laughing face
How many secrets it holds.
At my young age, how many
shadows of pain have I...'

Ranjeet, 15 years.

'Sow a small sapling,
and it will grow into a tree.
Light a small lamp,
and you will eliminate darkness.
If you place one brick on top of another,
you will build a palace.
If you speak kindly,
you will create a sense of oneness.
One good deed at a time,
will build a strong nation.

'नन्हा बीज एक बो दो,
वही पेड़ बन जाएगा।
छोटा—सा तुम दीप जला दो,
अंधकार मिट जाएगा।
अगर ईंट पर ईंट रखो तुम,
वही महल बन जाएगा।
मीठे बोल अगर बोलो तुम,
अपनापन बढ़ जाएगा।
अच्छे—अच्छे काम करो तो
देश बड़ा हो जाएगा।'

Shweta, 13 years.

SHAHANA'S STORY

Shahana, 17 years.

Shahana lives in a *basti* in the heart of the city and deeply values her life despite its hardships. The daughter of an auto-rickshaw driver and an *aanganwadi* worker, she is studying for a bachelor's degree at one of the city's top universities. Simultaneously, she is involved with a programme conducted by a children's organisation that builds skills in multimedia and communication. Along with others her age, she has learned about creative writing, audio, films and animation – and has put together an exciting project on the history of the *basti* she lives in. She appreciates her association with the organisation; constantly exploring and learning. She wishes to earn for her family like her elder sister does.

Humans, by nature, cannot live alone.
They like living with their families.
They cannot live in isolation.
They need their family's love at every
step to move forward.

इंसान की फ़ितरत ऐसी है वह अकेला नहीं रह
सकता। वह अपने आस—पास अपने परिवार
वालों को देखना पसन्द करता है।
इंसान तन्हा अपनी जिंदगी नहीं गुज़ार सकता।
वह कदम—कदम पर अपने परिवार वालों के
प्यार के साथ आगे कदम बढ़ाता है।

One of my friends in school was called Shahina.

Whenever I went to her house, her *Abbu* would scold us for some reason or other. He would say, 'Girls should not laugh too much, they should speak softly.' I always found that strange to hear.

Shahina left school after Class 8. I continued visiting her at home. She began to wear a *burqah* after leaving school. Whenever I went to her place, either she herself or her family, would try and persuade me that girls should wear a *burqah*. I couldn't say anything to her family. So I decided not to go to Shahina's house again.

After I had passed Class 10, I bumped into Shahina one day. She insisted on taking me to her home. I found her father at home. He met me and enquired which class I was studying in. I told him I was in Class 11. He was very happy to hear that and said, 'My daughter couldn't complete her studies, at least you will.'

I was surprised to hear that. I wondered, earlier this man had spoken so differently, now his ideas seem to have changed.

My other friend was Heena. She dreamt of going everywhere, without any restrictions imposed on her. She wished to do as her heart pleased. She liked wearing all kinds of clothes. She didn't think much of the *burqah*.

Today Heena has become a doctor. And Shahina is married.

I have another special friend, who is older. I consider him my true friend. And he is none other than my *Abbu*. Isn't that amazing? I have always wondered if there is anyone who can speak about almost anything to his or her father?

If I ever have anything to share, however secret it may be, I always say it to *Abbu*. *Abbu* is the keeper of my secrets. He is also an old friend. He guides me on the right path.

अब्बू मेरे हमराज़ भी हैं और बड़े दोस्त भी हैं। मुझे अब्बू ठीक राय देते हैं ।

My *Abbu* is called Kallu Qureshi. He loves all of us very much. You might say that is the case with most parents. But my *Abbu* is not my real father; he is our stepfather.

Another family in our neighbourhood also has a stepfather. There is a huge difference between my *Abbu* and their *Abbu*. Their *Abbu* always beats his stepchildren – he screams, shouts and ruins the peace of the house. People don't believe me when I tell them that *Abbu* is not our real father. They say, 'You are lying, you resemble your father.' And it is true that I resemble my *Abbu*, as if he were my real father. His love is more precious than any treasure in the world.

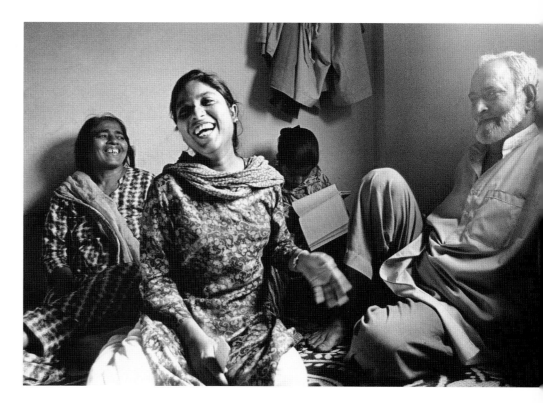

There are fights at home when we are short of money. Then I don't like anything at home. Similar sounds echo from all the houses around us. I am forced to ask why man has to run after money? Can't he do without it?

In her effort to look after us, *Ammi* has never been bothered about winter, summer or monsoon. Today she is inching towards old age. She needs to stay at home, but God has forgotten to assign rest in *Ammi's* fate.

अम्मी के नसीब में ऊपरवाला आराम लिखना भूल गया है ।

Earlier when there was no electricity in our *basti*, my brothers and sisters and
I would go to the *dhobighat* to watch TV. It was a little further from our *basti*.
We would rush there as soon as the sun set. Initially nobody at home knew that
we went to watch TV. But when *Abbu* found out he scolded us the first few times.
This didn't affect us. When we returned *Abbu's* stick would be waiting for us.
This scolding became part of our everyday routine, but we never gave up our habit.

Because of this, *Ammi* bought a TV. But there was no electricity, so how would the
TV work? *Abbu* bought a battery. The TV started working and we stopped making
our trips to the *dhobighat*.

Now when I look back and think of those days of watching TV at the *dhobighat*
and the beatings that followed, I wonder how strange childhood is! You are beaten
one minute and you forget the next. You are carefree as a child. You are not bothered
about your clothes or meals. In childhood, there is only you and your games.

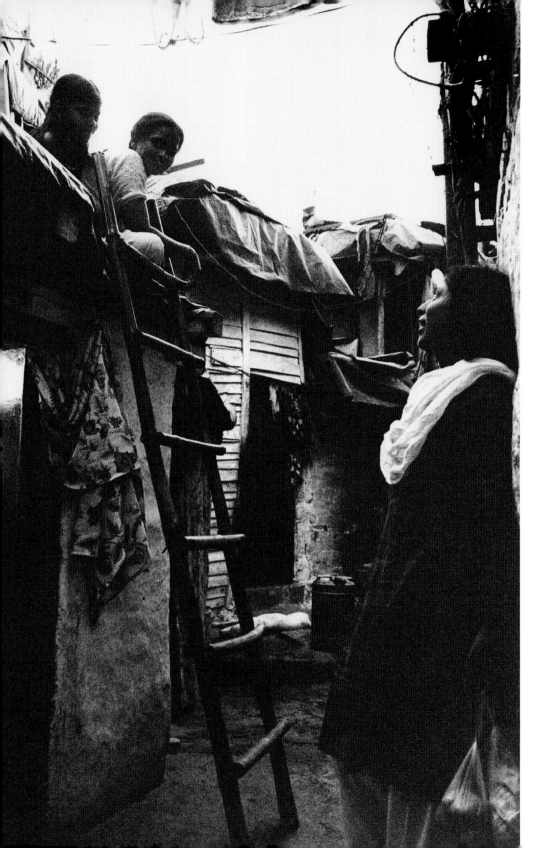

It is quite amazing how we all live under the same roof and yet have different ideas and feelings.

For example, I am a very fun loving person. I am always happy. If I have a problem, I get worried for a while but soon go back to being my happy self.

Shabana *baji* has a bad temper. Chand lives in his own world; not bothered about anyone. Israr, my younger brother, always feels that whatever he thinks and does is right.

All our habits are different, but we are pearls of the same necklace, strung together with love. These are the relationships that make us aware of our happiness and sorrow and enable us to share our joys and pains. If we didn't have the pillar of family bonds, our lives would have been similar to the lives of those living on footpaths.

Whenever *Ammi* asks my brother Chand for some money, he says, '*Ammi*, the situation at work is not too good. Only I know how I meet my family's expenses.' *Ammi* begins to worry and starts crying. When I see her tears I become furious with Chand and we start fighting.

I have just one wish – that I should be able to help *Ammi* with her expenses, just like my eldest sister, Shabana *baji*, does.

This world is vast. Different kinds of people reside in its every corner, followers of different religions and people from different castes. And so every human has a unique way of thinking. But people live together peacefully under one roof if they need to, even if the place is small. Their love binds them together.

When an earthquake occurs, there is no difference in the way it affects the house of a Hindu or a Muslim. Life and death are in the hands of Allah. Then why do we attempt to end each others lives?

If I ever fall in love with someone,
I will try and make him aware of my love.
I will tell my family about him and they
will support me. They have said,
'If you ever fall in love, let us know.
If the person is right for you, then we
will get you married to him.'
This is why I don't fear falling in love.
When my family is with me,
why should I be afraid of society?
Anyway the world is in the habit of
interfering in people's lives.

It is true that love is not intentional.
If it were, then we wouldn't hear of
love stories where the girl and boy
come from different religions, or where
a rich girl marries a poor boy.

That is why it is said:
'Pyar kiya nahin jaata, ho jaata hai.'

Earlier, when I met people I could only ask after their health. I was apprehensive
of asking anything more and getting to know them. What if they didn't like it?
What if it caused an argument? But now I can speak about anything to almost
anyone – a girl travelling on the bus or anyone else.

In the beginning when we started roaming around the *basti* with this video camera,
people would stop us and ask which television channel we had come from.
On which channel would they be seen? At that moment I felt that we had become
special despite being ordinary. In our own *basti*!

For transforming my life and expanding my world, credit goes to my friends at the
centre. If I hadn't come here, my world would have been limited to the four walls of
my house. I would never have known that I could write. ■

For children's participation, spaces and processes are required and must be created.
Spaces in which they can express their hardest challenges, their deepest desires
and their aspirations for opportunity and recognition; for freedom and friendship;
for basic needs, for dignity and non-discrimination.

'I would wish to study. I would wish that my father stopped doing drugs. And that happiness would light up our home.'

'मैं पढ़ना चाहूँगी। मेरे पापा नशा छोड़ दें। मेरे घर में खुशियाँ आ जाएँ।'

Soni, 10 Years.

'I would wish for every Indian to be educated. I would wish that every child receives a lot of love from their parents. And in the future I want more organisations to take care of boys and girls without parents, to never let them feel the loss. I want them to help these children build a future for themselves.'

Javed, 17 years.

'I would ask for the angel herself, a nice large home and good clothes.'

Harish, 12 years.

'I would ask for the development of slums, and for food, clothes and shelter, and the goodwill of God.'

Farida, 14 years.

'I would ask for a well paying job, a home and a lovely little girl child.'

Manju, 18 years.

'I would ask for happiness for my family. I would wish that I do well in my exams. And I would wish for the excitement of my birthday.'

Aarti, 13 years.

If an angel gave me three wishes...

'My first wish would be to become a cricket player. My second wish would be to arrange for an education for myself and others. My third wish would be to become a good human being and do something significant in the world.'

Krishna, 14 years.

'I would go to America and complete my studies. I want to go into space like Kalpana Chawla. And I would like to be able to join my family in their happiness.'

Bharti, 10 years.

'I would ask for education, a home and a brother.'

'हमे पढ़ाई और घर चाहिए। और एक भाई चाहिए।'

Shahana, 11 years.

'My three wishes would be to be completely healthy, beautiful and rich.'

Ashish, 13 years.

'I would wish to become a good human being and help the poor. I would like to feed my parents, sister and brother with my own earning. And I would like to educate the children who pick rags.'

'मैं अच्छा आदमी बनूँगा और गरीबों की सेवा करूँगा। और अपने माता-पिता, भाई-बहन को कमाकर खिलाऊँगा। और मैं उन बच्चों को पढ़ाऊँगा जो इस वक्त कबाड़ी बीनते हैं।'

Eid Mubarakh, 12 years.

'I would like to go to Paris in an aeroplane because it has all the facilities and comfort.'

Zaheera, 12 years.

'I would go to Mumbai with an angel. We would fly together, holding hands. And I would meet all the actors and actresses.'

Harish, 12 years.

'I would fly in a rocket to see the stars from close by.'

Mukta, 14 years.

'I would like to see the world from space and understand the significance of stars.'

'मैं अंतरिक्ष से पूरी दुनिया देखना चाहूँगी, सितारों का क्या महत्व है, वह सब देखना चाहूँगी।'

Saba, 11 years.

If I were given a free ticket...

'I want to go to two places – Saudi Arabia and Paris. I will soak in all the beauty of Paris and store it in my mind, never to forget it. I want to see snow falling. I will make snowballs and play with them. I want to go in an aeroplane.'

Fauzana, 10 years.

'I would like to go to Disney World by aeroplane to meet Mickey Mouse and Donald Duck.'

Monty, 12 years.

Neeta, 15 years.

Bina, 11 years

Our participation lies in our ability to support, invest and engage in programmes and organisations all over the country that are working to bring children closer to the fulfillment of their potential.

'I see myself as a college student.'

Ashish, 13 years.

'I see myself as a computer teacher in a big school, earning money.'

Mukta, 14 years.

'I will have grown older and will be going to a bigger school. I will have more friends. I will make everyone in my home happy. I will be beautiful and have a happy nature.'

Rani, 12 years.

Five years from now…

'I see myself as a professional cameraman and living in a house of my own.'

Pawan, 18 years.

'I see myself living in a big house. My looks and personality will have changed. I'll start off with a good job and then move on to business.'

Monty, 12 years.

'I will be 18 years old. I will be doing a course in painting and learning computers. And I will do exactly as I please.'

Sapna, 13 years.

'I would make a very big sea in front of my house because then I wouldn't have to spend money going to the sea.
I would make an airport near my house because otherwise I have to travel far. And I would be able to meet my *Nani* anytime without having to spend money.'

Zeinab, 12 years.

'I would show an honest way to thieves and robbers. I would educate all women.'

Soni, 10 Years.

'I would make all the poor rich.
I would give every poor person a decent place to live and I will make my teacher a millionaire.

Mukta, 14 years.

If I had the power to change the world ...

'I would remove hatred and hostility from the world. I would give a house to those who live on the streets and food to poor children.'

Jaitoon, 11 years.

'If I had the power I would make a flyover on every road. And I would make an airport in my neighbourhood.'

Rani, 12 years.

'I would put an end to discrimination and completely wipe out dishonesty and unemployment.'

Shikha, 15 years.

'I would reduce the prices of food grains and then build homes for all the poor people. I would reduce the cost of telephone calls considerably.'

Nazma, 14 years.

'I would change the politicians, the slums and the government schools.'

Saba, 11 years.

'I would give food, clothes and a home to all those who are poor or those who beg. I would put all the people who ill treat the poor and all terrorists behind bars and sentence them to death.
And I would beat all the greedy people and politicians to teach them a good lesson.'

Aarti, 13 years.

'I would end unemployment, crime and poverty. Because unemployment leads to poverty and poverty leads to crime. If the unemployed find work, then poverty will be contained.
As poverty reduces, crime will be contained too.'

Pravin, 18 years.

'I would eradicate all slums, ensure that rag pickers study and I would change people's eating habits.'

Rachna, 11 years.

'I would give equal rights and opportunities to women as men enjoy today. I would eradicate poverty. And I would resolve the Kashmir and Babri Masjid issues.'

Fauzana, 17 years.

'I would make all the cars fly in the sky because I don't like traffic. If I had the power I would not allow drugs to be made in this world. If I had the power I would not let myself grow old; I would like to remain a child.'

Rashida, 12 years.

'I would turn dirt and filth to cleanliness. I would wipe out poverty from India. And remove unemployment because it is a curse and the nation cannot progress as long as it exists.'

Amjad, 11 years.

Bina, 11 years.

Our participation lies in our walking the bridge

to a place that celebrates children

for who they are,

as they are

and who they might become.

LOVE
puts an end to all discrimination

Not so long ago, we would encounter open, blatant discrimination with signs like 'Indians and dogs not allowed' or 'For whites only'. Today, such flagrant discrimination would create a furor. But, is it really extinct? Or has it mutated into something more subtle? Isn't the existence of millions of people born without hope, living deprived childhood's, struggling to exist, enough proof that the ravages of exclusion are still prevalent?

Looking back at history where once discrimination was institutionalised, it is apparent that societies have been transformed. Our gods, our leaders and our poets have strived ceaselessly to create a utopia of equality and though they might not have been wholly successful, they have lifted many barriers. Unfortunately, violence and war have been the instruments popularly used to bring about a meaningful, systematic change. But there is a better way. Two great leaders come to mind: Martin Luther King and Mahatma Gandhi who spread their message, through love and peace resulting in revolutionary reforms. Their actions against two of the greatest evils of discrimination, racism and colonialism negated the widely held belief that violence was a handmaiden of change.

When we use love to spread a message it gives people a chance to wake up every morning with hope in their hearts, where they are not shut out because of race, gender, colour, economic status or religion. It creates compassion and opportunity. Love has no boundaries; it is unlimited, universal. Love breeds tolerance and peace. And most importantly, it unites.

It is only with this sense of unity that we can begin to address discrimination and its effects on society. A conscious shift in thinking is needed where we all recognise that as a part of humanity, we are not isolated and detached creatures on this planet. A feeling of unity will make us responsible human beings, remove indifferences and apathy. As a collective voice, we can raise and question issues; address what is amiss and change all that is unfair. We therefore need a process that will allow us to transform, to embrace all that we fear. To touch all that we do not understand.

After reading through the pages of this book, we can clearly see how children's organisations have been successful in developing a method that will allow a child the opportunity for a wholesome growth – a sense of security, access to education and specialised skills, cultural exposure, a chance to express opinions, develop friendships, play, dream, hope... the chance to belong. Individually and collectively we can attempt to narrow the divide by working with organisations that offer opportunities for participation.

As individuals, support to such organisations can be provided in terms of imparting academic, creative, professional and physical skills where we work towards strengthening the environment that will bring nourishment to a child's soul. Sponsorships, donating materials, building a playground, teaching vocational skills, changing mindsets that will allow children to learn and earn are some realistic solutions to enable meaningful change. Other possibilities include enhancing skills of staff members, conducting issue-based workshops and improving overall infrastructure. Interacting with children's organisations places us at the centre of the problem and here, we have the opportunity to meet the child and interpret her hardship, her vulnerability, and her creativity.

It is here where we could find the space to listen and follow the voice that speaks within our heart.

Similarly, how often do we stop to question encroachments and demolitions within our communities? We rarely allow ourselves to imagine the psychological damage of a bulldozer! What if they were our homes being destroyed, our children having to witness the rubble? We need to question ourselves; the law and its implementation. We need to research issues and mobilise the community into advocacy. We can familiarise ourselves with these issues by contacting grassroots organisations and perhaps then be a conduit to influence governance. A simple phone call can change mindsets, a quick letter can make healthcare accessible, an article on physical abuse, child labour and exploitation can generate mass scale awareness.

For collective participation, we could find opportunities within our areas of work.

Corporate Social Responsibility is a term widely used these days and companies are developing their own models of participation based on their own vision. The existing network of children's organisations is a simple channel where projects can be implemented, monitored, evaluated and sustained. Volunteerism, donations, skill building, vocational training and creating sustainable infrastructures within workers communities are often part of the CSR model.

The options are endless but if every individual inculcates a desire to make a difference, we can collectively and consciously engage our time in supporting programmes and children's organisations that attempt to bridge the gap and disconnection in our society. That every action is governed by love in order to ensure every child an equal opportunity – to survive, to develop and participate. To offer protection from the biases, intolerances, prejudices, segregation, favouritism and inequality that they encounter. To respect the beauty that lies within the silence of despair and recognise that a child... is a child... is a child.

It is only then can we hope to have a cultural shift in thought where perhaps within the appearance of opposites there is a sense of unity.

A true celebration of spirits.
United.

Leena Labroo
Senior Manager, Youthreach

चाँद तारों को छूने कि आशा

Children of Karm Marg.

the children

Aarti, 13 years
Aarti lives with her mother and siblings in a small slum dwelling. Her mother sells fruit at the nearby market. Aarti goes to a learning centre that has recently started in her community. She is very good at painting and would like to paint on garments.

Amjad, 11 years
Amjad has a disability and escaped from home as he was constantly being teased. He came to the city and worked in a store. While working he got in touch with a non-profit centre, where he now studies. He wishes to be honest and rich and serve his country.

Anil, 13 years
Anil's father threw him out of home at his step-mother's insistence. He landed on the streets and met with workers from a welfare organisation. He now enjoys living at their shelter and treasures his chance meeting with them. He wants to spread the message of love to his fellow beings.

Anil, 18 years
Anil is a mentally challenged artist. He now studies at a centre for special children where he enjoys sketching and painting a lot. He loves the centre and has imbibed a strong sense of self-reliance.

Anuj, 13 years
Anuj left home following his father's remarriage and subsequent ill treatment by his step-mother. He sweeps the streets for a living and lives with his friend's family in a slum dwelling. He dreams of becoming an honest policeman.

Asif, 14 years
Asif worked as help during weddings. Whenever he returned home late, he was severely beaten. He fled from home to end up on the city streets and picks rags for a living. He admires people who can converse in fluent English. He would like to become a dancer.

Ashish, 13 years
Ashish has recently begun to read and write with the encouragement of the children's organisation in his neighbourhood. He loves his music classes and wants to go to college. He nurtures a dream of becoming a pop star some day.

Atul, 15 years
Atul currently lives and studies at a shelter and picks rags in the day to earn a living. Having lost his parents at a very young age, he lived with his siblings at his uncle's home. He fled from the incessant beatings of his uncle and aunt. He aspires to become a social worker.

Azra, 16 years
One of 4 siblings, Azra comes from a conservative family. She has started visiting a learning centre run by a children's organisation in their community, against her father's wishes. She has now become an intrinsic part of the centre and has been officially appointed caretaker of the place. She would like to one day become the editor of a magazine.

Bharati, 10 years
Bharati was sent to a shelter for girls by her parents because of the paucity of funds at home. Here she goes to a public school and is very fond of watching programmes on science and technology. She dreams of becoming a cosmonaut.

Bina, 11 years
Bina's father is a tailor. Her family came to the city in search of a better livelihood. They live in one of the slum communities on the outskirts of Delhi. She looks forward to being married and having a family of her own.

Chanda, 14 years
Chanda, led a hard life as she lost her parents at an early age and was forced to live with her uncle in Uttar Pradesh. She was ill treated by him and ran away to the city. She washes utensils at a shop and lives with a group of children on the streets. She dreams of going to school like other children of her age.

Deepa, 15 years

Deepa is a hearing impaired artist, studying in Class 8 at an oral school for deaf children. She was born deaf due to the absence of the tympanic nerve, which carries vibrations from the ear to the brain. Her parents discovered this when she was two and so they decided to train her at a special school, enabling her to live in mainstream society.

Dhanraj, 15 years

Dhanraj is a hearing impaired artist. He lost his hearing partially following a severe beating by his schoolteacher when he was in Class 5. His parents then sent him to a special care school. He is a very promising child. Besides painting he enjoys listening to music with the help of his hearing aid.

Dilshad, 11 years

Dilshad's father ran a small grocery store in the *basti*. They were uprooted and sent to a faraway place as part of a demolition and beautification drive. Due to this, the family income dwindled and he had to give up his education. He dreams of becoming a college graduate and finding a respectable job.

Dinesh, 16 years

Dinesh ran away from home a number of times. He would run into constant arguments with his family members because of his carefree nature. He enjoys living at the shelter amongst his peers. He is good at working the computer, marketing and accounts and he looks forward to setting up his own business in the near future.

Eid Mubarakh, 12 years

Eid's father is a factory worker and his mother works at a local crèche. He studies at the street school run by the local welfare organisation. He loves his family and would like to do well in life to support them.

Farida, 14 years

Farida's family had built a home for themselves in the slum. Recently the civic authorities razed the structures to the ground and they were forced to find shelter elsewhere. They now live in a makeshift home, working hard to make ends meet. She has found work as a bangle maker. It hurts her to see her family in hardship and prays that they are able to re-establish themselves very soon.

Fauzana, 10 years

Fauzana lives with her mother and 2 sisters. Her mother weaves baskets to earn for the family and educate the girls. She looks forward to her classes in school as it keeps her away from the boredom of house chores. She dreams of becoming a teacher in her community.

Fauzana, 17 years

Fauzana comes from a family of potters. She had to give up studying after passing Class 10 due to shortage of funds at home. She is very involved with a non-profit organisation in her neighbourhood. Dynamic by nature, she actively participates in educating young girls in her community.

Firdaus, 13 years

Firdaus was compelled to work as part-time help in households in order to support her family income. She respects her mother for working hard to make ends meet especially due to her father's absence. Her dream is to study and earn a lot of money so that she can help improve the conditions of her home.

Gulnaaz, 12 years

Gulnaaz lives with her family of 7 in a large slum community. Her father runs a warehouse on the ground floor of their two-storied house. She studies at the local school. She would like to improve the conditions around her house and make everyone in her neighbourhood aware of cleanliness.

Harish, 12 years

Harish, very fond of his family, lives with them in a *basti*. His father holds a bachelor degree and encourages Harish to go to school. He is fond of studying and enjoys sports. He is a patriot and wants to become a soldier.

Jairam, 15 years

Following the demise of his parents, Jairam left home to avoid the never-ending fights with his brother and grandparents and came to the city. He works long hours at a tea stall by the station. He plans to give up drugs and start a new life.

Jaitoon, 11 years

Jaitoon lives with his parents and younger sister. His mother works hard to look after the 2 children as there is no support from the alcoholic father. Jaitoon goes to the learning centre in the community. He would like to travel the world to meet all poor children like him and see how he can make a difference.

Javed, 17 years

The son of a watchman, Javed ran away from his village. In the city he worked at a tea stall for a few months before coming to a children's organisation for shelter and schooling. Having finished school, he wishes to pursue a course in multimedia from a reputed IT institution and become proficient in English.

Jayanti, 14 years

Jayanti, along with her mother and brother, lives in a *basti* in the city. Following a demolition drive by the civic authorities, they were displaced from their original home. Her mother, a children's organisation worker, now has to travel a long distance and the cost eats into 70-80% of the household income. Jayanti would like to grow up and become a pilot and travel around the world.

Jwalamukhi, 12 years

The son of a cobbler, Jwalamukhi was forced to work and earn money for the household. His parents refused to send him to school. He ran away from home and arrived at a city railway station. He chose to live on the platform because he found access to basic amenities and above all, found companionship. He would like to go to Disneyland with his friends.

Krishna, 14 years

Krishna lives with his family in a slum community. He gave up studies at an early age and was put to work at a carpentry shop. In his available leisure time he enjoys playing cricket in his neighbourhood. He would like to become a cricketer.

Manju, 18 years

Manju comes from a conservative family. She has shed her inhibitions and recently started learning at the centre run by a children's organisation in her locality. Having mastered the skill of operating computers she now looks forward to a bright future.

Manoj, 15 years

Manoj lost his family during a fair in the city. Left alone, Manoj worked in a city motel to take care of himself. He aspires to become the Prime Minister of the country. He would then ban all children from working and make learning compulsory.

Mehrunissa, 13 years

Mehrunissa's family faced extreme hardship during the communal riots. Her father drives an auto rickshaw and mother sells vegetables. She wants to learn the computer and be self-reliant. She doesn't want to be married at a young age.

Mohit, 14 years

One of 2 siblings, Mohit is a mentally challenged boy. He studies at a school for the mentally deficient in the city. A confident boy, he studies in Class 3. He loves Maths and English. He is very attached to his family and teachers and is especially close to his younger brother.

Monty, 12 years

Monty lives with his relatives in the city. His parents sent him away from the village so he could get a good education. Monty excels in sports more than his studies. He dream is to become a famous cricketer.

Mukta, 14 years

Living in a makeshift house with her 2 brothers and sister, Mukta goes to school at the insistence of the local organisation. She wants to change her place of living, as it is unhygienic. She would like to become a dietician.

Naushad, 11 years

The eldest of 7 siblings, Naushad lives in one of the largest slum colonies in Delhi. Here he helps his father in their tailoring shop as well as goes to school. His favourite subject is Maths and he is happiest when he ranks first in class.

Naveen, 18 years

Naveen came to the city to escape his father's beatings. He was immediately taken in by a non-profit organisation where he currently studies in Class 10. He has also completed a course in electronic repairs. He dreams of setting up his own business one day.

Nazma, 14 years

Nazma's parents till a small piece of land in the village. They sent her to live with relatives in the city. She was moved by the endless sea of poverty that plagues the large cities and would like to work towards the betterment of people living in difficult circumstances.

Neelofar, 15 years

The eldest of 4 siblings, Neelofar lives with her family in a one-room house. Having given up her formal schooling after Class 10, she is now learning computer skills at a non-profit centre. She enjoys writing her thoughts eloquently and providing clarity to others' ideas.

Neeta, 15 years

Neeta, a vibrant girl, began to face difficulties at an early age in understanding and keeping up with what her teachers taught in class. Her parents soon discovered that she was a slow learner and could not keep up with activities children her age engage in. She now studies at a learning centre for special children and is regaining her confidence.

Neha, 13 years

Neha lives with her family in a slum dwelling. Her father sells vegetables while her mother makes handicrafts at home. Street educators approached her parents to allow Neha a chance to study. She is currently being educated at the local centre run by the organisation. She sees herself as growing up to be a businesswoman and working after she is married.

Pawan, 18 years

Due to his aversion to working in fields, he left his home for the city. Here he found a shelter that would help him realise his dreams. Besides going to school he is also fond of photography. He has started working as an apprentice with a photographer in the city.

Pravin, 18 years

Floods devastated his home and family because of which he came to seek shelter at a welfare centre. He now pursues his education at a government school. He would like to lead a meaningful, busy and independent life. He wishes to become an actor or director in the future.

Rachna, 11 years

Rachna lives in a one-room house with a family of 8 members. She has to pick rags to supplement the household income. As a girl, she faces a hard life as a rag picker. She nurtures a dream of going to school one day.

Raju, 12 years

After running away from home due to severe shortage of funds, Raju found himself on the pavement. He picked rags with a group of other boys in order to earn a living. They live in constant fear of the police and their beatings. He dreams of becoming a lawyer for child rights.

Rakesh, 10 years

Rakesh got lost on an outing with his father. He travelled from Calcutta to Delhi and repeatedly tried to go back to his family. He started picking water bottles at the New Delhi railway station and now works as a porter. He dreams of travelling by train and being united with his family.

Rani, 12 years

Rani lives with her unemployed father and grandmother. She is very close to her grandmother who encourages her to study. She would like to finish college and find a job to establish herself and support her family.

Ranjit, 12 years

Tired of going to the *Madrasa* school where he was caned regularly by his teacher, Ranjit left his family of 9 members and ran away. He came to the city and started working at a grocery store. He dreams of earning a lot of money and leading a comfortable life.

Ranjeet, 15 years

Cruelly treated by his stepmother after his father's death, Ranjit ran away from his home in Bihar at the age of 7. He lived on the platform at the New Delhi railway station for several years. Finally he took refuge in a children's shelter which today, he proudly calls his home. He attends school regularly and loves being with animals and people.

Rashida, 12 years

Rashida lives with her mother and drug addict father. She wishes her father would give up drugs and work to ease the family's crisis for funds. Rashida works in homes to help her mother with the family income. She would like to go to a big school and become an intelligent, loving person.

Rohit, 15 years

In order to add to his family income, Rohit began working at a large stationery shop in the heart of the city. Although he has to carry heavy loads through the day, he looks forward to his work as it keeps him busy. He dreams of becoming an artist.

Saba, 11 years

Saba lives with her mother and 3 brothers. She misses her father as he passed away recently. She daydreams of outer space and would like to become an astronaut.

Santosh 13 years

Santosh came from a family of farmers and was ill treated by his stepmother. Forced to leave his village, he came to the city to look for odd jobs on the streets and make a living for himself. He aspires to earn enough to build a house and lead a happy life.

Sapna, 13 years

A free spirit, Sapna had the courage to leave home and come to the city. Fortunately for her she came in contact with a girls' organisation soon after arriving and has lived with them. She is a keen learner and aspires to fulfil her dreams in the future.

Shahana, 11 years

Shahana comes from a family of *qawwals*. She lost her brother recently in a road accident and is now afraid of crossing roads. If she gets an opportunity, she would like to become a doctor. She wants all women to be educated so that they can fight for their rights and bravely face every difficulty in life.

Shariful, 13 years

Shariful and his 2 younger brothers were forced to work as *bidi* makers after their father lost his job as a factory worker. He yearns for his father to find a job so that he can go back to leading the life of a 13 year old.

Shikha, 15 years

Shikha, second in the line of 5 siblings, lives with her family in a slum in the city. She is very close to her family and goes to a government school with her siblings. She loves studying and would like to become a navy officer.

Shweta, 13 years

Shweta lives in a *basti* in the city with her parents. Her father works in a hardware store and her mother is a housewife. She got in touch with an organisation through her neighbours. She would like to become an administrative officer because she would then have the power to make a difference.

Soni, 10 years

Soni dreads living at home as she is subjected to bitter fights because her father is a drug addict. She would like to clean up her surroundings and dreams of becoming a social worker.

Sumitra, 12 years

Their grandmother brought up Sumitra and her siblings, as both parents were alcoholics. One day, their slum was demolished and they ended up at a non-profit shelter. Sumitra's roommates call her 'laraku viman' (fighter plane). She believes in mutual respect between human beings and justice.

Sunita, 12 years

Sunita lived with her family of 6 in a slum community in the city. She used to go to a nearby school. After the Municipal Corporation moved them away from the city and rehabilitated them to an erstwhile dumping ground, she was forced to give up her schooling and attend to house chores. She has to fetch water from a distant well, as the only water available is from stagnating pools and open drains. She would like to resume her studies soon and become a lawyer.

Suresh, 13 years

His alcoholic father regularly beat Suresh and his mother. He ran away from home and eventually met someone at the railway station who offered him protection at the centre. He currently goes to school and studies hard to fulfill his dream of becoming a police officer so he can protect his country.

Sushil, 12 years

Having recently arrived in the city, Sushil has made friends with a group of boys at the railway station. He has begun to pick used bottles to make a living. Still trying to get used to the hardships of city life, he dreams of finding security, a well-paid job and a roof over his head.

Tabassum, 13 years

Tabassum was devastated after having lost her siblings in a fire. She studies in Class 2 at the local school and looks forward to meeting her friends everyday. She wishes to make a difference in the lives of children and old people.

Zaheera, 12 years

Zaheera lives with a loving family in a slum dwelling, amidst a lot of din and clutter. She would like to lead a life away from the noise, go to school and learn tailoring. She plans to earn well and find her family a better place to live.

Zeinab, 12 years

Zeinab's mother was recently arrested at the border, while crossing over from a neighbouring country. Although her father is around, she misses her mother a lot. Given an opportunity, she would like to become a doctor.

Zubaid, 12 years

Zubaid lived with his family in a makeshift slum community. The authorities decided to rid the city of such habitation and Zubaid was removed to a distant place, 30 kilometres away from his old school. His commute takes him a good two hours by bus and at times when the buses don't run on time, he reaches home late at night. He dreams of becoming a businessman and building a big house in the heart of the city.

sharing rain

The human reality that underlies the pictures and words in the preceding pages of the book speaks for itself. Those who have helped give voice to this reality in the book cannot know what feelings it has evoked in you who read it. But for some of us, as for some of you, the deep beauty and pain of it may have seemed just overwhelming.

As we emerge from the world in these pages, as we see a reflection in these human souls of those we ourselves love…brothers, sisters, sons and daughters who could so easily have been where they are…it's almost too much to understand or bear. Some of us would have felt numbed by the vulnerability of the children into whose eyes we look and whose words we read. Seeing their humanity as our own, we may despair about our ability to help them. Understanding the magnitude and scale of the problem, we may feel paralysed.

This book was created to ask you to join us in listening, not to that fear and despair, but rather to the love and sense of hope that resides in many of our hearts, just below the surface. We, at Youthreach, passionately believe that the reality that takes away dignity and freedom, safety and love from countless children around our country can be changed, that the beauty, strength and potential of these children can be unleashed. All it will need is that we do not turn our faces away, that we do not walk the other way. All we need is to look at the truth and reach out to it with love. For while there are millions of street and slum children, there are also millions of us. In the last fifty-six years India too has changed and grown. Tens, if not hundreds, of millions of Indians today have the resources to reach out in some way to those around us who live without livelihoods and freedom.

Our experience at Youthreach gives us deep hope. Over the years, hundreds of people have joined us in connecting the ever-growing resources of the private sector to the many, effective organisations that work to transform the lives of street and slum children. Through the work of these NGOs and others like them throughout the country, tens of thousands of children have already been given security and love, education, healthcare, livelihoods and hope. There are many cases where, having benefited from all of this, these children have returned to work with their own communities to allow others to share the resources and opportunities that they themselves were given. And this is of course only the beginning.

At Youthreach we pledge ourselves to being the very best channel we can be to serve you and help you reach out in whichever way you wish to or are able to. Please let us help you reach out. Or find another manner to engage with the reality that speaks through these pages. Whether we succeed or fail together in this mission depends not so much whether this book touched our hearts…but rather whether each one of us chooses, in whichever way is appropriate, to translate that feeling into action.

These children dream of 'being the rain'.
We need not dream.
Each one of us could be the rain for them, bringing life-giving water.
And that very rain would fall softly on the driest places of our own hearts.

Uday Khemka
President, Youthreach

youthreach

Founded in 1997, Youthreach is an endeavour to create a connection between worlds, through direct participation and change.

Youthreach strives to instill in each one of us a sense of collective responsibility in addressing social issues. We create projects within our core programmes that enable young people to contribute their time, energy and skills that would benefit and strengthen grassroots organisations working with disadvantaged children and environmental issues.

Awareness Creation Programme focuses on gradually building awareness through dissemination of information and sensitisation on issues related to disadvantaged children, the environment and women.

Volunteer Programme matches your skills and interests with needs of organisations in the city; coordinating from the start to the completion of every individual interaction and project.

Bridging with Corporates promotes philanthropy among large companies and corporations.

Saturday School works with a large group of children every Saturday afternoon at a local school in Okhla, where we attempt to supplement the children's school curriculum through non-formal education.

University Programme partners with Pravah to help support social sensitisation initiatives in colleges.

Youthreach Grants offer financial support to children's organisations through its own corpus and through funds given by corporations and individuals.

The underlying ethos of Youthreach is the belief that we as individuals greatly enrich our lives by giving back to the larger community we live in and draw from so abundantly.

Because we believe, no matter who you are or how much time you have, together we can make the difference.

Our Partner Organisations working with Children

Delhi: Aashray Adhikar Abhiyan • Action for Autism • Adhaar Welfare Society • Akshay Pratishthan •Ankur Society for Alternatives in Education •Association for Cricket for the Blind • Butterflies • Deepalaya • Divya Chaya Trust • Hope Foundation • Hope Project • Karm Marg • Literacy India • Mobile Créches • National Association for the Blind, Delhi • National Association for the Blind, India • Navjyoti Delhi Police Foundation • Project WHY • Sahan • Salaam Baalak Trust • Udayam Prayas • Udayan Care • Very Special Arts • VIDYA • Vidya & Child

Bangalore: Hope Foundation • Chandigarh: Pustak • Kolkata: Future Hope • Mumbai: Akanksha Foundation, Oasis, Helen Keller Institute for Deaf and Deaf Blind • Uttaranchal: Aarohi

what you can do

If you are an individual

- Share your time and experience with children living in, or associated with children's organisations.
- Sensitise your friends and family about children leading hard lives.
- Impart professional skills in the field of medicine, law, counselling, architecture, etc.
- Offer creative skills by painting murals, designing websites, conducting workshops on photography, art, pottery, origami, etc.
- Provide apprenticeship to children for a year or more in sculpture, dance, music, theatre, photography, fine art, etc.
- Enhance the skills of staff at our partner organisations by conducting workshops on administration, teaching, communication, leadership, counselling, finance, human resources etc.
- Spread awareness within your community on issues such as child rights, literacy, shelter and demolitions.
- Help mobilise materials from friends, schools and colleges that can be distributed to our partner organisations.
- Sponsor a school or a child's education, medical care, and nutrition.
- Organise fund raising events.
- Design an income generation programme with a clear business plan to help older children use their skills to earn a livelihood.
- Write proposals to donor organisations to help raise funds towards a project or organisation.
- Provide strategic inputs to organisations.
- Be creative – think of your own imaginative ways to help out.

If you are a business house or corporation

- Develop a Corporate Social Responsibility model for your organisation.
- Impart skills and training to staff of children's organisations.
- Provide long-term solutions at the community level.
- Host interactive sports tournaments.
- Invite children to your factory or organisation for an educational field trip.
- Sponsor a child or a school's infrastructure.
- Promote Children's Hour – Donate an hour's salary of every employee towards a project. Alternatively, give a certain percentage of your company's turnover towards a children's project.
- Donate surplus goods.

If you are an educational or professional institution

- Impart teaching skills to the staff of organisations.
- Allow children access to your facilities – space, sports grounds, laboratories, computers.
- Spread awareness on issues such as child labour, child rights, shelter, etc.
- Collect materials and books for distribution.
- Sponsor a child.
- Provide children with the opportunity to get admission at your institution.
- Subsidise educational courses.
- Provide access to health check-ups.
- Subsidise doctors' fees, medical examinations, medicines, and surgeries.
- Organise health camps i.e. ENT, maternity care, general health, etc.

If you are a media house

- Sponsor articles, columns on issues affecting the lives of disadvantaged children.
- Air talk shows, interviews, and messages to generate public opinion.
- Sensitise audiences by screening short films on the lives of children.
- Sponsor space for posters in order to facilitate awareness.
- Create opportunities for older children to learn skills in the area of journalism, multimedia, etc.
- Invite children for field visits.

Please call us at Youthreach for more details.
Ask for Anubha, Prerna or Shveta.
Phone 91-11-2653 3520 / 25 / 30

There are times when I am happy
and times when I am not so happy.
That's when I am sad.
I have to be happy to make a drawing.

I read and write. I hurt my head and so my
hair was shaved off. It's good in the summer.

I am standing with flowers in my hand
waiting to be photographed.

Ranjit, 12 years.

the photographers

our gratitude

'If I were rain' was made possible by your invaluable support.

A.K. Sood
A.S. Negi
Achinto
Akanksha Foundation
Amar Behl
Amit Khullar
Andrew Sharp
Anita Khemka
Ankita Anand
Ankur Choksi
Ankur Society For Alternatives in Education
Arjun Sawhney
Arti Kalkat
Arun Ganguly
Asahi India Glass Ltd.
Asha Narayan
Azad A Bhutia
Ballarpur Industries Ltd.
Benu & Ramji Bharany
Bharat Kapur
Bharat Kharbanda
Butterflies
Chanda Narang
Charudutt Chitrak
David de Souza
Dayanita Singh
Deborah Ingham
Deepalaya
Devika Singh
Devika Daulat Singh

Dhruv Singh
Divya Kashyap
Ed Millbank
Fawzan Hussain
First City Magazine
Fisheye Design
Gauri
Gautam Thapar
Grand Hyatt
Gurinder Osan
H.S. Bedi
Henry Ledlie
Hope Project
IDP Education Australia
Imran Baig
Imaging Solutions
Indu Prakash Singh
Interglobe
Jane Blaffer Owen
Jason Taylor
Jaya Srivastava
Karm Marg
Kavita Charanji
Khemka Group
Mahuya Banerjee
Maithili Kumar
Manjari Sharma
Manish Swarup
Manoj Jain
Martin Auer
Mita S

Mona Schwartz
Myra Macdonald
Nanhi Kali
Navjyoti Delhi Police Foundation
Neeraj Paul
Niraja Nanjudan
Niti Sabharwal
Nitin Upadhyay
Old World Hospitality
Pablo Bartholomew
PhotoInk
Prabhat Kumar Jha
Pradeep Dasgupta
Praveen Nair
Priyanka Dasgupta
Project WHY
Punj Lloyd Ltd.
Rashmi Khattar
Reuters
Ritu Singh
Roma Sinai Mukherjee
Rotary Club of Delhi, Southend
SV Photographics
Salaam Baalak Trust
Samar Jodha
Sandeep Mani
Sanjay Acharya
Sanjay Labroo
Sanjiv Saith
Sanjoy Chatterjee
Sanjoy Narayan

Santosh Verma
Saroj Bishnoi
Sautam Mukherjee
Shalini Sharma Rattan
Sharat Bhagat
Sheyna Baig
Shipra Ogra
Shivali Jain
Sona Koyo Steerings Ltd.
Sondeep Shankar
Sonia Poddar
Sudeshna Chatterjee
Sunjay Kapur
Sunny Narang
Swapan Parekh
Tanya & Arvind Dubash
Tarun Chhabra
Tina Tahiliani Parikh
Thomson Press
Uditangshu Mehta
UNICEF
Urvashi Khemka
Veena
Very Special Arts
Vijay Bhargav
Vijay Jodha
Vivek Sarin
Vinay Jain
Yashpal
Zuber Aria

glossary

Aanganwadi	– Local Créche		*Hanuman Mandir*	– A Hindu place of worship
Abbu	– Father in Urdu			
Ahimsa	– Non-violence		*Ibarat*	– Text
Almirah	– Cupboard		*Id*	– A Muslim Festival
Ammi	– Mother in Urdu			
			Kheer	– Indian dessert made from rice and milk.
Baba	– Father or grandfather			
Baji	– Older sister in Urdu		*Lal Quila*	– The Red Fort in New Delhi
Basti	– Slum community		*Langra*	– Lame, handicapped
Beta	– Son			
Bhai	– Brother		*Madrasa*	– A college for Islamic instruction
Bhaiya ji	– Elder brother		*Mehndi*	– Henna, the leaves of a plant that yields colour, used to beautify hands or colour hair
Bharat	– India			
Bidi	– Smoking tobacco rolled in a leaf		*Murrie*	– Puffed rice
Burqah	– Veil, part of the traditional Islamic clothing for women			
			Nana	– Maternal grandfather
			Nani	– Maternal grandmother
Chachaji/ Chacha	– Father's brother			
Charas	– Hashish, an intoxicating herb		*Paan*	– Betel leaves
Chawal	– Rice		*Pulav*	– Rice cooked with vegetables
Coolies	– Porters working at railway stations			
			Qawwals	– Singers of Muslim devotional songs
Dadaji	– Paternal grandfather			
Dhabas	– Street side eating places in India		*Ram*	– The central character of the Indian epic *The Ramayana*
Dharamshala	– Public inn, a house for pilgrims			
Dhobighat	– Laundry area by a water source			
Didi	– Older sister		*Sabzi*	– Vegetables
Diwali	– An Indian festival of lights		*Salwar Kameez*	– A traditional two piece Indian outfit
Dussehra	– An Indian festival		*Sevaiya*	– Indian dessert made with vermicelli cooked in milk
Ganja	– Leaves and buds of the hemp plant, smoked for intoxication; grass; weed		*Shaktiman*	– Mythological god of might and power
Gulab Jamuns	– An Indian sweet meat		*Taal*	– A kind of palm tree found in the coastal areas of India
Gutka	– Chewable tobacco			

sources of information

Books and Papers

Aashray Adhikar Abhiyan: *The Capital's Homeless.* New Delhi, 2001.

Association for Development: *A Study on the Problems of Street and Working Children in Delhi.* New Delhi, 2002.

Butterflies: *Bal Mazdoor ki Awaaz.* New Delhi, 2000-03.

CRY: *The Indian Child.* Mumbai, 1999.

CRY: *The Indian Child.* Mumbai, 2001.

Foundation for Humanization: *Humanscape Magazine.* Mumbai, 2000-03.

HAQ: Centre for Child Rights: *Children in Globalising India: Challenging our Conscience.* New Delhi, 2002.

IMRB: *Slum, Street and Working Children in Delhi: A Situational Analysis.* New Delhi, 2000.

Rita Panicker: *Working and Street Children in Delhi.* National Labour Institute, New Delhi, 1992.

Rita Panicker and Kalpana Desai: *Street Girls of Delhi.* National Labour Institute, New Delhi, 1993.

UNICEF: *The State of the World's Children.* New York, 2002.

United Nations: *Convention on the Rights of the Child.* New York, 1989.

Individuals and Organisations

Deepalaya, New Delhi.

Devika Singh, Forces, New Delhi.

Global March against Child Labour, New Delhi.

Indu Prakash Singh, Aashray Adhikar Abhiyan, New Delhi.

Lara Shankar, New Delhi.

Martin Graham, Future Hope, Kolkata.

Praveen Nair, Salaam Balak Trust, New Delhi.

South Asian Coalition against Child Servitude, New Delhi.

Tarun Chhabra, New Delhi.